In Loving Memory
"Pretty Girl"
Tammy Butler

September 12, 2004

Our phenomenal success in real estate investing is from the support, confidence, enthusiasm, encouragement, commitment, love, and sacrifice during 21 wonderful years with the "Pretty Girl" who allowed me to "break my chain" to invest aggressively and safely. Most investors can only dream of having a life partner and soul mate so perfect.

Warning: This Material is Copyright Protected.

PUBLISHED BY:
Wealth Building 24-7 LLC & Vista Software Inc.
4012 Dupont Circle, Suite 203
Louisville, KY 40207
(502) 896-2595   www.VistaSoftwareInc.com

DISCLAIMER AND/OR LEGAL NOTICES:
While all attempts have been made to verify information provided in this manual and its associated ancillary materials, neither the Authors nor the Publisher assumes any responsibility for errors, inaccuracies or omissions. Any slights of people or organizations are unintentional. If advice concerning legal or related matters is needed, the services of a qualified professional should be sought.

This manual and/or its associated ancillary materials are not intended for use as a source of legal or accounting advice. Also, some suggestions made in this manual and/or its associated ancillary materials concerning marketing, product sales, or referral fees, etc., may have inadvertently introduced practices deemed unlawful in certain states and municipalities. You should be aware of the various laws governing business transactions or other business practices in your particular geographic location.

Any references to any person or business, whether living or dead, existing or defunct, is purely coincidental.

PRINTED IN THE UNITED STATES OF AMERICA

	User Registration

Congratulations!
Register Online 24hrs

Investor Books
24 Hour ONLINE Registration
At
www.MikeButler.com/UserRegistration.htm

Or You Can Mail to:
Wealth Building 24-7 LLC of Ky.
P.O. Box 24181
Louisville, KY 40224
Office Hours: 8am-3:30pm EST
(502) 896-2595
This is the phone number to our real estate office (Vista Properties, Inc.)

PLEASE COPY This Form & PRINT LEGIBLY

Buyer Name: _____

Company: _____

Address: _____

City, St. Zip:_____

Phone: (____)_____ Fax: (____)_____

I'm using QB Pro Version: _____

Authorized User #1:_____

Authorized User #2:_____

(Confidential: Number of Units):_____

My Email: _____

My website: _____

Enter Your User Registration Serial Number:_____

(found on your Valid User Certificate located on inside cover)

Where did you buy your **INVESTOR BOOKS?**_____

1   *User Registration*

2   *Mike Butler*

3   *J. Michael Grinnan CPA*

              & McCauley Nicolas & Company LLC

4   Intuit QuickBooks Pro®

5   **Installing- "Restoring" Your CD**

6   **"RESTORING" Investor Books CD**

7   **"RESTORING" (install) your CD – Where is it?**

8   **"RESTORING" (install) your CD – Step 2**

9   "RESTORING" (install) your CD – Step 2

10   Getting Started- User ID and Password

11   **NEW Speed Buttons**
in QB Pro 2006!

12   Back up – put it on your computer AND a CD

13   Getting Started- User ID and Password

14

15   # Beginner Basics

16   Accounting – 4 Basic Types of Accounts

17   Accounting KISS Method – Balance Sheet

18   Accounting KISS Method – Profit & Loss

19   Accounting – POST OFFICE, Walls of Types of Accounts.

20   Accounting KISS Method – Money between Boxes

21   Accounting – Post Office Boxes Income & Expenses

22   QB Pro HELP – is Great, use it for routine stuff

23   Sorting DATA – How QB sorts Data

24   Sorting DATA – Property Examples

25   Sorting DATA – Property with Numbered Streets

26   Sorting DATA, - Property Examples

27   Sorting DATA – Examples of DATES

28 Sorting DATA, Example – TEST - PRACTICE

29 Sorting DATA – PRACTICE TEST ANSWERS

30 **Sorting DATA, Chart of Accounts - Real Estate**

31 Sorting DATA, Chart of Accounts - Bank Accts.

32 Sorting DATA, Accounts - Mortgage Loans

33 Beginner Basics - Sorting DATA, ground rule MUST

34 Beginner Basics - Types of Accounts - Balance Sheet Definitions

35 Beginner Basics - Chart of Accounts - Income and Expense Definitions

36 Beginner Basics - Income & Expenses Fit into IRS Schedule E

37 Income & Expense Accounts vs. Schedule E

38 Fast Review Chart of Accounts Structure - Bank Accounts

39 Chart of Accounts Structure - Escrows

40 Beginner Basics - Chart of Accounts Structure – Equipment (Asset)

41 Beginner Basics - Chart of Accounts Structure - REAL ESTATE (Asset)

42 Beginner Basics - Chart of Accounts Structure – VEHICLES (Asset)

43 Beginner Basics - Chart of Accounts Structure - Money Loaned (Asset)

44 Beginner Basics - Chart of Accounts Structure - CREDIT CARDs (liability)

45 CASH FROM ME

46 Chart of Accounts – MORTGAGES (liability)

47 Chart of Accounts - INCOME & EXPENSE – WHY?

48 Chart of Accounts Structure - INCOME & EXPENSE

49 Beginner Basics - Chart of Accounts Structure – Broker Income, Insurance

50 Beginner Basics - Chart of Accounts Structure – INCOME INTEREST

51 Beginner Basics - Chart of Accounts Structure –Rent INCOME – Sale of Asset

52 Beginner Basics - Chart of Accounts Structure - COGS

53 Chart of Accounts Structure - INCOME & EXPENSE

54 Chart of Accounts Structure - INCOME & EXPENSE

55 Beginner Basics - Chart of Accounts Structure – CAPITALIZED EXPENSE

56 Beginner Basics - Chart of Accounts Structure – Equipment EXPENSE

57 Beginner Basics - Chart of Accounts Structure – Mortgage Interest EXPENSE

58   Beginner Basics - Chart of Accounts Structure – RENT EXPENSE

59   Beginner Basics - QB Pro - "MEMO" Field

60   Getting Started - first desktop view

61   Getting Started - first desktop view – Reminders Window

62   Getting Started - Desk Top View

63   Getting Started - first desktop view - TOOLBAR

64   Desk Top View – TOOLBAR w/Drop Downs

65   SPEED BUTTONS

66   SPEED BUTTON - create a CHECK

67   SPEED BUTTON - Registers

68   **SPEED BUTTON – Credit Cards including Personal Purchases**

69   Chart of Accounts - CREDIT CARDs (liability)

70   Speed Button - ENTER BILLS

71   Speed Button PAY BILLS

72   Speed Button PAY BILLS

73   Speed Button – VENDOR (before 2006)

74   Speed Button – VENDOR (Pro 2006 Users)

75   Speed Button - VENDOR - Set Up New

76   **VENDOR** - Set Up New - 1099 Independent Contractor

77   **1099s**

78   Speed Button - Account

79   Speed Button - Reminders

80   Speed Button - To Do

81   Speed Button - MEMORIZED TRANSACTIONS

82   Speed Button - **DEPOSIT**

83   Speed Button –
      REPORTS

84   Accounts - Income & Expense - CLASS

85   **"CLASS" Feature** *makes it sing*

86   Cartoon of CLASS, Post Office Boxes

87   Profit and Loss by CLASS Report

88   Create Your Chart of Accounts

89   **Enter Your Bank Accounts**

90   Entering Your Bank Accounts

91   Entering Your Bank Accounts

92   Entering Your Properties

93   Setting up Your Properties as Fixed Assets

94   Setting up Your Properties w CLASSES

95   CLASS - Setting up properties - CLASSES

96   SINGLE MEMBER LLCs

97   Setting up properties - CLASSES w/ LLCs

98   LLCs (less than 20 properties example)

99   w/ LLCs (More than 20 properties)

100   EARNEST MONEY (Good Faith Deposit)

101   EARNEST MONEY for Buying - the check

102   # Closing Statements

103   Real (HUD 1) Example - What is going on

104   Closing Statement- Where to Start

105   Closing Statement - KISS Cartoon - Cash Purchase

106   Cartoon - Cash Purchase, Tenant occupied

107   Cartoon - Cash Purchase, Tenant occupied, EARNEST MONEY

108   Cartoon - Purchase w/ Loan, Tenant occupied, & EARNEST MONEY

109   Cartoon - Purchase w/ Loan, Tenant occupied, & EARNEST MONEY

110   Closing Statement - CASH Purchase

111   **BUYING - CASH Purchase**

112   Closing Statement - CASH Purchase

113   CASH Purchase - enter CLASS

114   CASH Purchase - enter CLASS

115   CASH Purchase - What is going on

116   CASH Purchase

117   CASH Purchase

118   CASH Purchase

119   CASH Purchase - Back Page

120   CASH Purchase - Front Page

121   CASH Purchase - Front Page

122   CASH Purchase - Front Page

123   CASH Purchase - Front Page

124   CASH Purchase - Front Page

125   CASH Purchase - Front Page

126   CASH Purchase

127   CASH Purchase

128   CASH Purchase

129   CASH Purchase w EARNEST MONEY

130   **Cash Out Refi (or Buy with Loan)**

131   Cash Out Refi - set up accounts

132   Cash Out Refi - set up liability acct

133   Cash Out Refi - set up liability acct

134   Cash Out Refi - set up liability acct

135   Cash Out Refi - new liability account

136   Cash Out Refi - new liability account

137   Cash Out Refi - new liability account

138   Cash Out Refi - new liability account

139   **Cash Out Refinance w/Escrow**

140   Cash Out Refinance w/Escrow

141   Cash Out Refi w/Escrow

142   Cash Out Refi w/Escrow

143   Cash Out Refi w/Escrow

144 Cash Out Refi w/Escrow

145 Cash Out Refi w/Escrow

146 Cash Out Refi w/Escrow

147 Cash Out Refi w/Escrow

148 Cash Out Refi w/Escrow

149 Cash Out Refi w/Escrow

150 Cash Out Refi w/Escrow

151 Cash Out Refi w/Escrow

152 Cash Out Refi w/Escrow

153 Cash Out Refi w/Escrow

154 Cash Out Refi w/Escrow

155 Cash Out Refi w/Escrow

156 Cash Out Refi w/Escrow

157 **Cash Out Refi w/Escrow – w/ Old Loan**

158 Refi - Set Up Mortgage Payment

159 Refi - Set Up Mortgage Payment

160 Refi - Set Up Mortgage Payment

161 Refi Set Up Mortgage Payment- PRINCIPAL PAID

162 Refi - Set Up Mortgage Payment

163 Refi - Set Up Mortgage Payment

164 Refi - Set Up Mortgage Payment

165 Refi - Set Up Mortgage Payment

166 Refi - Set Up Mortgage Payment

167 Refi - Set Up Mortgage Payment

168 Refi - Set Up Mortgage Payment

169 Refi - Set Up Mortgage Payment

170 Refi - Set Up Mortgage Payment for Auto Pay

171 Refi - Set Up Mortgage Payment for Auto Pay

172 **Selling – Closing Statements**

173 Closing Statement- Selling has 3 Steps

174   Cartoon - Closing Statement when SELLING

175   SELLING -pay off mortgage, Tenant occupied

176   SELLING - (Contract f Deed, 1st, 2nd Mtg)

177   Selling Step 1 - Cash Deal

178   Selling Step 1 - Cash Deal

179   Selling Step 1 - Cash Deal

180   Selling - Step 2 for Every Sale

181   Selling - Step 2 for Every Sale

182   Selling - Step 2 for Every Sale

183   Selling - Step 2 for Every Sale

184   Step 3 Every Sale- Edit CLASS

185   Step 2 for Every Sale

186   Step 2 for Every Sale

187   Cash Deal, Pay Off Mortgage

188   Step 1 - Installment SALE

189   SALE Step 1 - Installment SALE - new asset acct

190   Installment SALE - year end report result

191   SALE Step 1 - w/ tenant, & more etc.

192   ESCROWS - paying Taxes & Insurance

193   RETURNED CHECKS

194   Security Deposits

Many investors get totally bamboozled, confused and frustrated in dealing with a Tenant's Security Deposit because we are told this is not our money. This is your Tenant's money we are holding just in case they damage any of part of property above normal wear and tear....

THIS Language is probably from your LANDLORD/TENANT LAW and NOT the IRS!

The IRS does NOT give a flying rat's kahoona about your local landlord tenant law!

195   OPTION MONEY

- **Many Investors pull their hair out on this one too.**

- **Let's keep it simple.**

- **USE YOUR IRA HAT HERE...**
- **Ask Yourself:**
  - **– Did You Sell This Property?**
- **ANSWER IS NO!!! (not yet)**

196 ▦ **Creating CHECK to Tenant**

197 ▦ Creating CHECK to Tenant

198 ▦ CHECK to Tenant **REFUND Security Deposit**

199 ▦ **BUYING NOTES & Mortgages**

200 ▦ **1031 Tax Deferred Exchange**

201 ▦ SELLING - 1031 Tax Deferred Exchange

202 ▦ 1031 Tax Deferred Exchange

203 ▦ 1031 Tax Deferred Exchange

204 ▦ 1031 Tax Deferred Exchange

205 ▦ 1031 – STEP 2, ZERO out SOLD ASSET

206 ▦ 1031- STEP 3 - Edit the CLASS

207 ▦ 1031 – STEP 3 Edit Class

208 ▦ 1031 Tax Deferred Exchange – BUYING new Property

209 ▦ 1031 Tax Deferred Exchange – BUYING new Property

210 ▦ Cartoon - Buying with 1031 Exchange funds

211 ▦ 1031 Tax Deferred Exchange - Buying

212 ▦ 1031 Tax Deferred Exchange

213 ▦ 1031 Tax Deferred Exchange

214 ▦ 1031 Tax Deferred Exchange

215 ▦ 1031 Tax Deferred Exchange

216 ▦ 1031 Tax Deferred Exchange

217 ▦ 1031 Tax Deferred Exchange

218 ▦ **DEPRECIATION**

219 ▦ DEPRECIATION – Doing it Yourself

220 ▦ DEPRECIATION – Doing it Yourself

221 ▦ DEPRECIATION – Doing it Yourself

222 DEPRECIATION – Doing it Yourself

223 DEPRECIATION – Automatic Monthly Entry

224 DEPRECIATION – Automatic Monthly Entry

225 DEPRECIATION – Automatic Monthly Entry

226 DEPRECIATION – Automatic Monthly Entry

227 **Year End - THINGS TO DO**

228 **Year End - Principal Pay Downs**

229 **Year End - 1st Step with CPA**

230 *Year End* - Last Step with CPA

231 *Make it do MORE – Things You should learn.*

232 *Make it do MORE – Things You should learn.*

233 **Common Questions & Answers**

234 **Common Questions & Answers**

235 **Resources**

Louisville Police ID Photo, March 2000

Mike Butler

- raised Louisville, Kentucky
- Oldest of 7 children
- bought 1st house before 20
- married 20 years, 2 daughters
- Very active in local REIA
- Retired early *(due to Real Estate)*
- Undercover Police Detective,
Handicap? My Full Time Job....

- **Money** magazine, June 2001,
- "Can Real Estate Make You Rich?
- Author #1 Best Seller on Amazon
- "Landlording On AutoPilot"

Mike was raised in Louisville, Kentucky and is the oldest of 7 kids. He bought his first house before age 20. In 1991, while buying another rental house, Mike met Ed Melton Sr., who introduced him to the Kentuckiana Real Estate Investors Association. From KREIA and by attending workshops and seminars around the country, Mike developed into a focused, aggressive real estate investor, who takes pride in avoiding banks to buy investment property. He's still very active in KREIA today.

Mike realized early on he MUST have a strong foundation in order to grow quickly and *safely*. Mike has reviewed many property management software programs only to discover they fell short of what he needed. Remember, property management software is usually designed for those who manage property for others for a fee. Those programs can cost thousands of dollars plus more for tech support. Mike has spent and invested THOUSANDS of hours developing the 5M VISTA Software Powered Wealth Auto Pilot System using QuickBooks Pro®. His system gets results.

He enjoys teaching and helping fellow investors; however, with so many requests, he decided to kill 8 birds with one rock and create courses to show fellow investors how to use these programs to suit each investor's individual needs. HIs 3 Day "Make Your 1st Million" , Webinars, Chalk Talks, and Coaching Program ,landlording, and the monthly Cranking It 24-7 members are helping investors everywhere!

With Tenant Tracking™ and Investor Books™, you'll have fewer headaches, nightmares, and expenses. You'll increase your profit and will be able to spend more time on what you want to do in life.

Successful investing utilizing his effective Tenant Tracking and bookkeeping techniques enabled Mike to retire in March 2000 after 13 years as a Louisville Police Detective.

Mike was featured Money magazine, June 2001, in the article "Can Real Estate Make You Rich?" and the Wall Street Journal Radio Show syndicated to over 170 radio stations.

Mike authored "Landlording on Auto-Pilot" published by John Wiley and Sons and made the #1 Best Sellers List on Amazon.com Get your copy today and get Free Forms at from the special website.

He's a Kentucky licensed real estate broker, member of KREE (Kentucky Real Estate Exchangers), and a charter member of the local chapter of NARPM (National Association of Residential Property Managers), Past President of KREIA (Kentuckiana Real Estate Investors Association).

Mike thanks his family for their support and confidence. Special thanks to the Kentuckiana Real Estate Investors Assn. He attributes much of his success to this association.

KNOWLEDGE IS POWERFUL!
Your Education Should NEVER STOP!

J. Michael Grinnan CPA
& McCauley Nicolas & Company LLC

"The Real Estate Investor's CPA"

McCauley Nicolas & Company LLC
702 North Shore Drive, Suite 500
Jeffersonville, IN 47150
(812) 288-6621
E-mail: mike_grinnan@mnccpa.com

"It's absolutely incredible what Mike Butler has done. He's achieved the impossible by creating an autopilot wealth creation system making it possible for Mom and Pop investors to own 10, 20, or more properties while having more free time than they ever thought possible. His system based on icons and non-technical language that even a computer illiterate can rapidly master, allows investors to enjoy the wealth and lifestyle they always dreamed of"

J. Michael Grinnan CPA

Intuit QuickBooks Pro®

- **Intuit's QuickBooks Pro® is an accounting software program.**

- **It will be referenced by "QB" & "QB Pro"**

- **Screenshots are from QB Pro.**

- **Some Procedures may not work on older versions.**

Like Riding A Bike; once learned, YOU CAN FLY!

STOP being a slave to some unique small software company.

Intuit is the maker of Quickbooks Pro.

Intuit makes the #1 accounting software program in America!

EVERY competent CPA and accounting firm uses Quickbooks.

This course along with Tenant Tracking uses Quickbooks Pro and you can STOP being a slave to the other software companies.

Quickbooks Pro does it ALL!

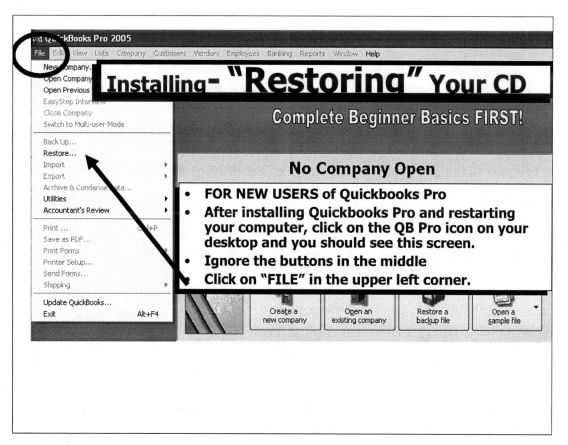

The easiest way to install Investor Books is to go to

www.mikebutler.com/restoring.htm
And follow the windows media player 6 minute tutorial

On Your CD There are TWO Back up Files in each folder – One is Labeled SAMPLE to use with this manual for training and easy reference. The other is completely clean, ready to go for you.

FINALLY, Congratulations! HERE YOU GO, Now you should be out of your comfortable chair and at your computer. Thank You for your patience, it will pay off. In order to make this as painless as possible, I hope you have read all the pages before this page. If not, please do so now.

This is the view new users of Quickbooks Pro will see.

If you already use Quickbooks, you will see a slightly different screen.

The objective here is to **"RESTORE"** your Investor Books file.

You can NOT simply open it.

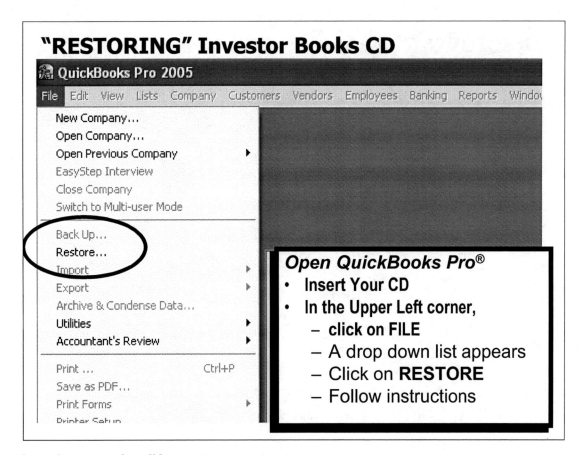

"RESTORING" Investor Books CD

Open QuickBooks Pro®
- **Insert Your CD**
- **In the Upper Left corner,**
  - **click on FILE**
  - A drop down list appears
  - Click on **RESTORE**
  - Follow instructions

The easiest way to install is to go to

www.mikebutler.com/restoring.htm

And follow the windows media player 6 minute tutorial

Be Careful Here – Please Read this.

You can NOT click on the file on the CD and get your Investor Books file to open. The file on your CD is a Quickbooks Company "BACK-UP" file. It is Intuit's way of compressing data to take up less space on a disk. You must "restore" the compressed back-up file first BEFORE you can use it.

This 'RESTORE' process involves 2 steps.

1.) You must tell Quickbooks where the file to be restored is located. Odds are it can be found on your CD drive.

2.) You must tell Quickbooks where to want to place the file AFTER it has been restored. I recommend to place it in a folder inside of "My Documents". This sets the stage for easy back up of ALL of your personal, business, and real estate data.

"RESTORING" (install) your CD – Where is it?

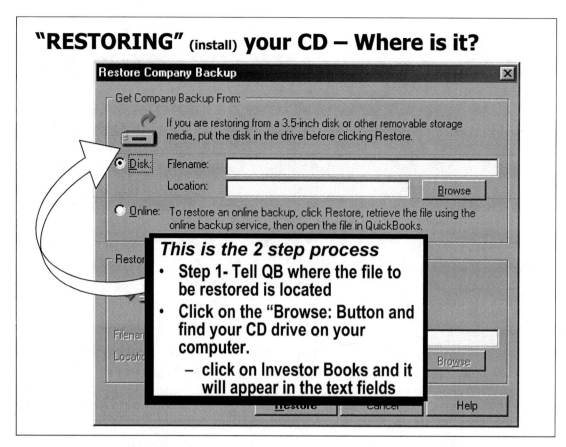

This is the 2 step process
- Step 1- Tell QB where the file to be restored is located
- Click on the "Browse: Button and find your CD drive on your computer.
  - click on Investor Books and it will appear in the text fields

The easiest way to install is to go to

www.mikebutler.com/restoring.htm

And follow the windows media player 6 minute tutorial

Shown below is what you'll see on your Investor Books CD.
- **The top folder are for QB Pro 2002, 2003, 2004 users**
- **Quickbooks Pro 2005 Users will open the Pro 2005 Folder**
- **QB Pro 2006 User will click and open the Pro06 Folder**

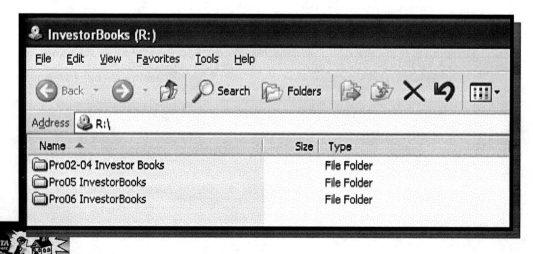

"RESTORING" (install) your CD – Step 2

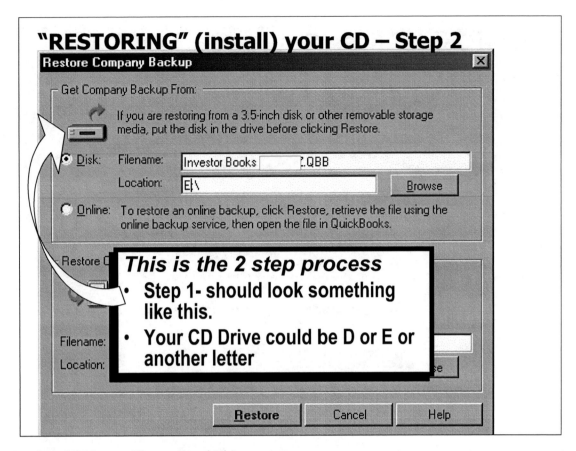

This is the 2 step process
- Step 1- should look something like this.
- Your CD Drive could be D or E or another letter

Be Careful Here – Please Read This

Shown Below is what QB Pro 2006 Users will see inside the folder.

There are two company files. Select one.

- a clean one named **Investor Books**

- sample file name **InvestorBooksSAMPLE**

> -Use the Sample file for training and refernce only. Do NOT plug your stuff in the sample file.

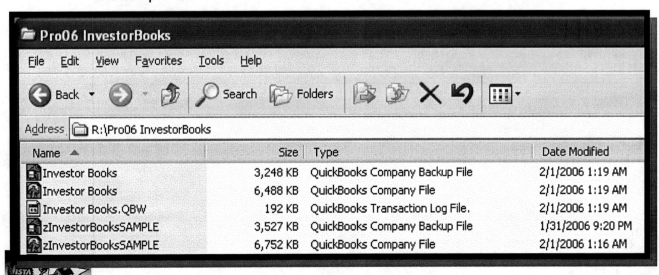

"RESTORING" (install) your CD – Step 2

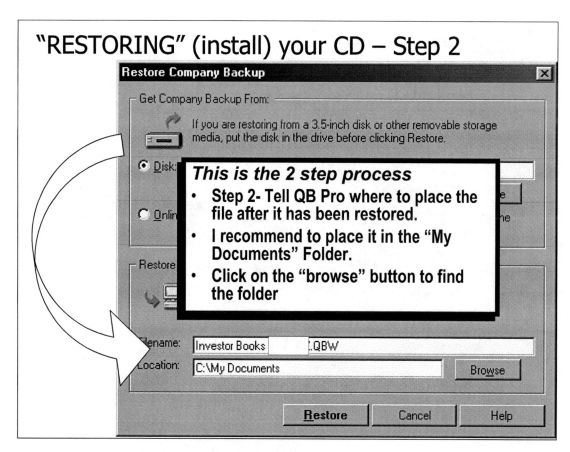

Be Careful Here – Please Read this.

Simply put, this "restore" process involves "uncompressing" a QB backup file and telling your computer where to install this new QB file. I highly recommend you place your Investor Books file somewhere in your "MY DOCUMENTS" folder to allow for easy back up of all of your data.

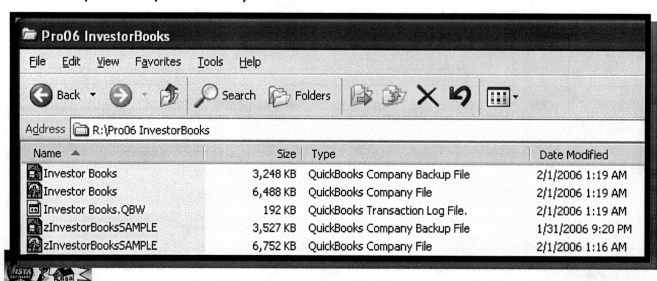

Getting Started- User ID and Password

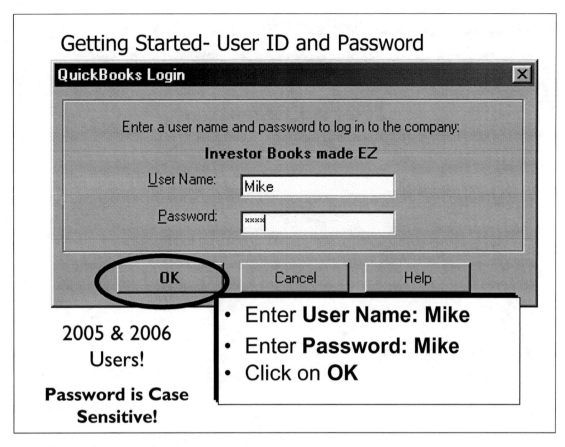

2005 & 2006 Users!

Password is Case Sensitive!

- Enter **User Name: Mike**
- Enter **Password: Mike**
- Click on **OK**

You will see this screen next.

Sometimes ADMIN will default and appear in the User Name field.

User Name: Mike
Password: Mike

Some versions of 2006 have   User ID: **mike**   Password: **mike**

Click on the OK button and your Investor Books Quickbooks Company File will open.

QB Pro 2005 users PASSWORD is Case Sensitive

Changing your User ID and Password.

If you wish to change it, go to the toolbar and select COMPANY.

A drop down list appears and select SET UP USERS.

Follow the steps and make your changes.

Remember, if you change these, ONLY YOU will know them. Write it down somewhere. If you lose it or forget it, you will have to call Quickbooks for help.

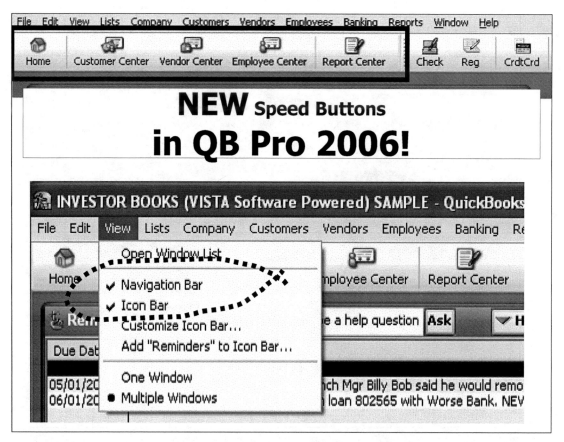

NEW In Quickbooks Pro 2006

If you are upgrading from an older version of QB into QB Pro 2006, The Speed Buttons (Icon Bar) located to the left of the CHECK Button will appear.

All of your Speed Buttons from the CHECK button to the right are the same as in all previous versions.

The Customer Center Button should NEVER be used in Investor Books; however, it will be the most frequently used button in Tenant Tracking.

REMOVE THESE BUTTONS:

1.) Click on the "VIEW" Button on your toolbar

2.) UNCHECK, remove the checkmark √ next to Navigation

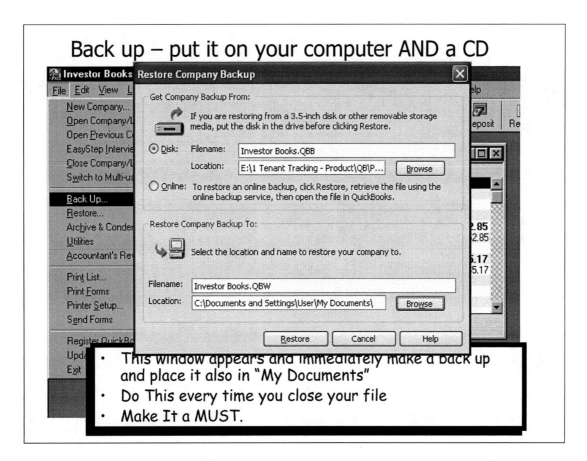

Back up – put it on your computer AND a CD

- This window appears and immediately make a back up and place it also in "My Documents"
- Do This every time you close your file
- Make It a MUST.

BACKING UP your Investor Books file

Back up to MY DOCUMENTS

Make another onto a CD or disk

Getting Started- User ID and Password

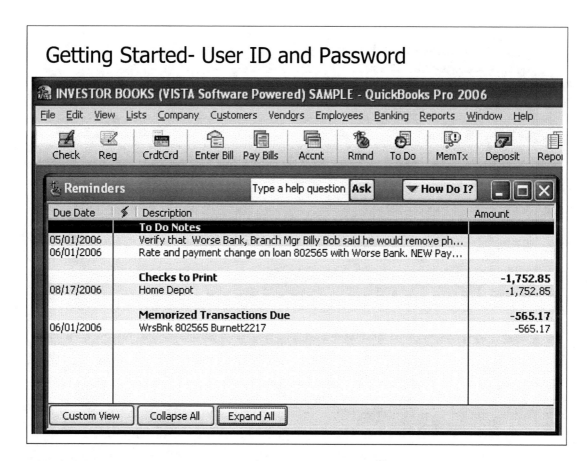

The first view of Investor Books.

There is sample data in this company file for you to reference the procedures displayed in this manual.

The SAMPLE transactions are dated in the 1930's to prevent them from mixing in with your transactions causing grief on your reports.

PLEASE Use the Investor Books SAMPLE file for TRAINING AND EASY REFERENCE

IMPORTANT: Make a Back Up Now and then email it to yourself for off site back up and storage.

Each entity filing a tax return must have it's own "set of books" not only for tax time, but for asset protection concerns. Investor Books allows you the most simple method and system of pulling this off without creating a boatload of extra work.

The fewer tax returns, the better as far as being organized and spending money on entities and tax prep fees.

Most experts encourage you to have a separate "company file" for each entity. Sure, they are right, but, they are doing their darnedest to get you to make things easier for them…, not you.

Here's the bottom line, if you can simply give them the information they want, sorted the way the want it (by entity), who cares how you get there…. I promise, it makes your life a whole lot easier operating day to

The IRS does NOT care how much your tenant owes you, what they tore up, how loud they play their music, etc. (so never give this info to your CPA, they won't turn off their meter while reviewing the useless stuff)

This system allows you to report income as you receive it BY PROPERTY.

Beginner Basics

Investor Books keeps track of your:
- – **Income and expenses**
- – **What you buy, sell, borrow, and loan.**
- • **QB Pro Tips**
  - – **uses many features EXCEPT Account Receivable**
  - – **You Will NOT bill customers here**
  - – **Tax Preparation with day to day operations**

Investor Books feature keeps track of what you buy, sell, borrow, and loan, PLUS your income and expenses.

Tenant Tracking keeps track of those folks who owe you money...

You will report income as you receive it. This is the true CASH method of accounting.

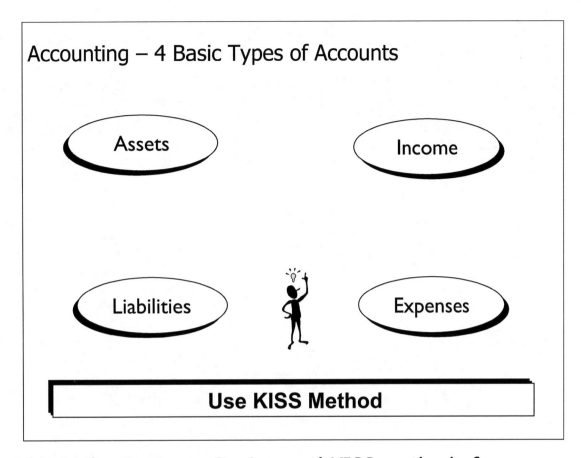

Accounting – 4 Basic Types of Accounts

Assets

Income

Liabilities

Expenses

Use KISS Method

This is the Beginner Basics, and KISS method of Accounting.

The basic simple version - 4 account types.

ASSET – things you own.

LIABILITIES – money you owe

INCOME – money coming in

EXPENSE – money going out.

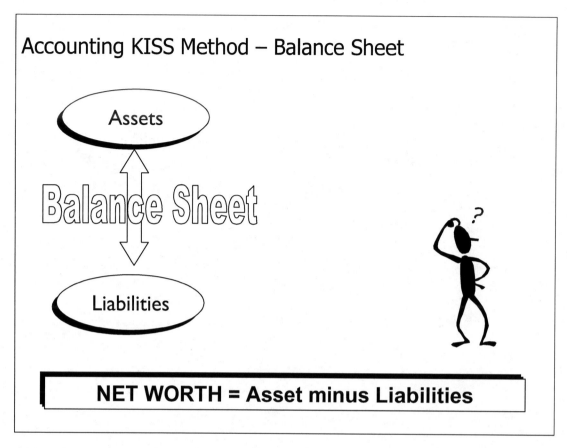

Accounting KISS Method – Balance Sheet

Assets

Balance Sheet

Liabilities

NET WORTH = Asset minus Liabilities

These two create your

BALANCE SHEET

They determine your net worth.

Real Estate you own are YOUR Assets

Money owed are YOUR Liabilities

Hopefully,
Assets minus Liabilities EQUALS A
POSITIVE NUMBER for your NET WORTH.

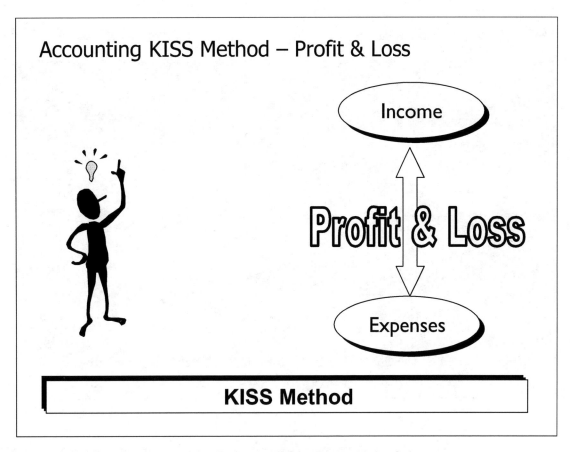

Accounting KISS Method – Profit & Loss

Income

Profit & Loss

Expenses

KISS Method

Profit and Loss Report is determined by the Total of the Income Accounts minus the total of the EXPENSES Account.

Hopefully, this is a positive number. Surprising, many investors have trouble with this BECAUSE OF ACCOUNTANTS or BOOKKEEPER.

Accountants and Bookkeepers TRAIN Investors to ignore profit and loss reports.

Many times their P&Ls are useless to the investor because the investor views it as a CASH FLOW report when it's really a Tax Summary Report.

This just adds to the stigma of the being labeled bean counters.

INVESTORS WANT REPORTS TO HELP INVESTORS!

Accounting – POST OFFICE, Walls of Types of Accounts.

Assets

Liabilities

Income

Expenses
(on another wall)

ALWAYS from an Account, ALWAYS into an Account

You are in a room with walls of accounts.

Each Wall is a Different type of account.

You have one wall for:

Assets

Liabilities

Income

Expenses

Money moves between the boxes.

The boxes are located on a wall

This is the SIMPLE guide to Accounting. It works.

You do NOT see any money on the floor... you can NOT use a MISC or general for a "dumping ground" for stuff.

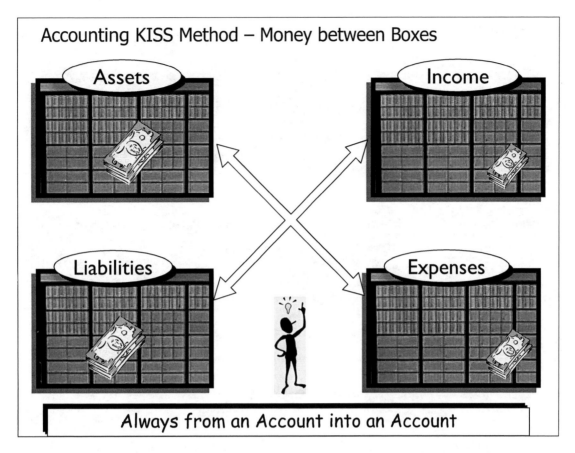

In simple transactions, money moves from one box to another box.

For example, writing a check from your bank account to pay for an electric bill is simply moving money from the bank account (asset wall) to the utility box found on the Expense wall.

Sometimes there are 2 or 3 step transactions. They still use this simple system.

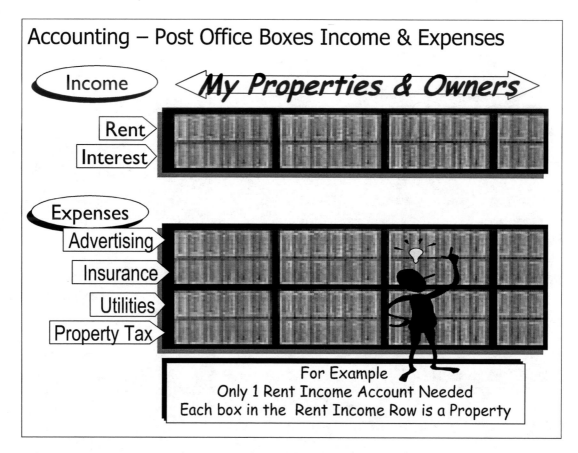

Accounting – Post Office Boxes Income & Expenses

Income

My Properties & Owners

Rent
Interest

Expenses
Advertising
Insurance
Utilities
Property Tax

For Example
Only 1 Rent Income Account Needed
Each box in the Rent Income Row is a Property

The above example shows PO Boxes.

The top 2 rows can be found on the INCOME WALL.

The bottom 4 rows are found on the EXPENSES WALL.

Each column represents a property you own. (this part is Quickbooks, we will cover it again later)

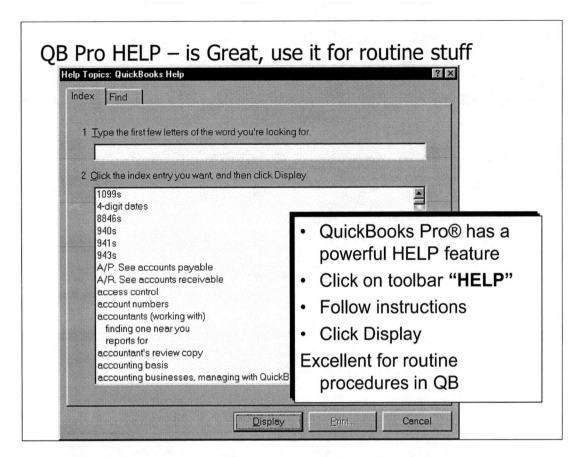

QB Pro HELP – is Great, use it for routine stuff

- QuickBooks Pro® has a powerful HELP feature
- Click on toolbar **"HELP"**
- Follow instructions
- Click Display

Excellent for routine procedures in QB

Quickbooks Pro has a powerful help feature.

USE IT. It works.

If you need help with a routine procedure (such as creating a check or balancing a bank account)

This help section is phenomenal.

Simply type in the word of the item you need help with and Quickbooks will take you there.

Sorting DATA – How QB sorts Data

- Ground Rule
- Data is sorted in many ways
- The most common is ALPHABETICALLY
  - Keep this in mind throughout all applications
  - In sorting data, numbers are placed before alphabet.
  - For example, let's have QB Pro sort the following:

    Hudson, Cat, 1, 34, 9, Midnight

    - Result equals

      1, 34, 9, Cat, Hudson, Midnight

  ## QB Pro sorts data this way!

Take a moment and think like a computer.

If you tell your corn pewtor to sort in order the above listed items – Look how it sorts them.

It sorts numerically first, then alphabetically.

It sees **H,C,1,3,9,M** and sorts them in this order to equal **1,3,9,C,H,M**

If this seems foreign, stop and review now.

Sorting DATA – Property Examples

- To sort properly, **must** use ground rules.
- For example, Houses below.
  - *6 houses to enter:*
    - 3215 Vermont Drive
    - 11612 Main St.
    - 165 N. 44th St.
    - 3345 New Cut Rd.
    - 2301 S. 4th St.
    - 1151 S. 9th St.

- Think in this format:
  - Vermont3215
  - Main11612
  - 44th165n
  - NewCut3345
  - 04th2301s
  - 09th1151s

<StreetName><HouseNumber><Direction>

Good, I hope you understand the previous screen. If you do not, GO BACK NOW.

Once understood, view the list above.

Begin NOW changing the way you identify property. NO EXCEPTIONS.

3215 Vermont Ave. is now Vermont3215

11612 Main is now Main123 and so on.

If your town has no more than 99 numbered streets, you must place a ZERO in front of the single digit numbered streets. If you live in a large town with over 100 number streets you must place TWO ZEROs in front of the single digit number streets in order for QB to sort properly.

Sorting DATA – Property with Numbered Streets

- After thinking in this format:
- Your data will be sorted properly
    - 3215 Vermont Drive
    - 11612 Main St.
    - 165 N. 44th St.
    - 3345 New Cut Rd.
    - 2301 S. 4th St.
    - 1151 S. 9th St.

RESULT:
- 04th2301s
- 09th1151s
- 44th165n
- Main11612
- NewCut3345
- Vermont3215

In order for 9th St to sort in front of 44th St.,
- You MUST place a ZERO in front of the 9.

Using the naming system properly, your properties will sort in order displayed in the RESULT window.

This BASIC rule of naming data is the foundation for both Tenant Tracking and Investor Books.

The sooner you master this way of thinking, the sooner this system actually becomes EASY... RIDING THE BIKE.

Sorting DATA, - Property Examples

- This ground rule is a MUST
- Used with properties, accounts, lenders, loans,..
- Practically every procedure with QB Pro involves this ground rule of sorting data.
- YOU MUST understand and apply this ground rule to make it work for YOU
- Major part of Building your foundation.

RESULT:
- 04th2301s
- 09th1151s
- 44th165n
- Main11612
- NewCut3345
- Vermont3215

To help reinforce this, let's try it on DATES....

This method of renaming or identifying STUFF is the foundation for your system.

Study it and understand what is going on before moving forward. It is used extensively.

It works on Properties, Bank Accounts, loans, dates, Tenants (in Tenant Tracking) Vendors, checks, etc, etc, etc,

Sorting DATA – Examples of DATES

- Let's sort in chronological order the following years:
  - **97, 98, 99, 00, 01, 02**
- It's easy to assume these are years in order; however, in your computer, the numbers will sort in this order….
  - **00, 01, 02, 97, 98, 99**
- Your computer sorted correctly & did **NOT** make a mistake!
- MUST format data properly
- Had data consisted of four digits, **1997, 1998, etc.** the results would be proper.

Data entered WRONG will be sorted WRONG....

The same system applies to dates.

THINK LIKE A CORN PEWTOR.

You and I both know if we see or say

97, 98, 99, 00, 01 we assume years and this appears chronological to you and me.

WRONG – your corn pewtor will sort it correctly and it will read 00, 01, 97, 98, 99.

In order to sort properly,

you MUST think FOUR DIGITS

1997, 1998, 1999, 2000, 2001, 2002 etc.

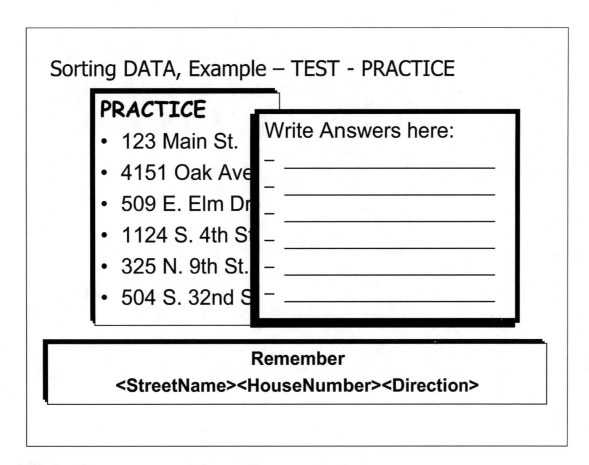

Sorting DATA, Example – TEST - PRACTICE

PRACTICE
- 123 Main St.
- 4151 Oak Ave
- 509 E. Elm Dr
- 1124 S. 4th St
- 325 N. 9th St.
- 504 S. 32nd S

Write Answers here:
- _____
- _____
- _____
- _____
- _____
- _____

Remember
<StreetName><HouseNumber><Direction>

This is a practice Screen.

Try it.

Write in your book here or on scrap paper

FOLLOW the format as displayed at the bottom of the above window. Use the space below if you wish for future training.

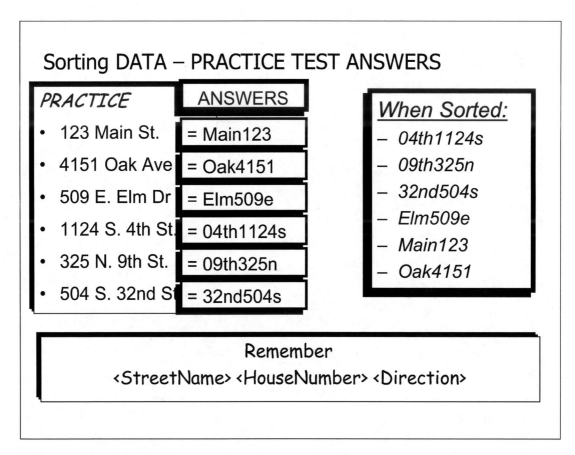

Sorting DATA – PRACTICE TEST ANSWERS

PRACTICE

- 123 Main St. = Main123
- 4151 Oak Ave = Oak4151
- 509 E. Elm Dr = Elm509e
- 1124 S. 4th St. = 04th1124s
- 325 N. 9th St. = 09th325n
- 504 S. 32nd St = 32nd504s

When Sorted:
- 04th1124s
- 09th325n
- 32nd504s
- Elm509e
- Main123
- Oak4151

Remember
<StreetName> <HouseNumber> <Direction>

Here is your answer. See it worked!

If something is wrong STUDY IT NOW.

Do NOT move forward.

Do NOT move past GO. STOP NOW until you get it right.

If you try to advance without having this down pat, this whole system will NOT work for you.

If you feel good about, let's move on.

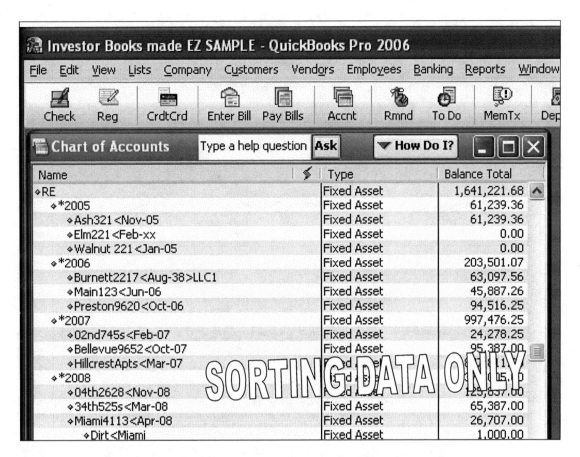

NO need to scroll thru list, just begin BANGING in street name

If more than 1 on same street, Quickly enter street name house

QB takes you straight to the Account!

Imagine having dozens or hundreds of properties.

Now could this be more powerful?

Suppose I wanted to see how much I had in my property at Main123.

To see my answer, I simply start banging in "Main12..." on my corn pewtor and QB takes me directly to the Main123 property and the black highlight lands on the property.

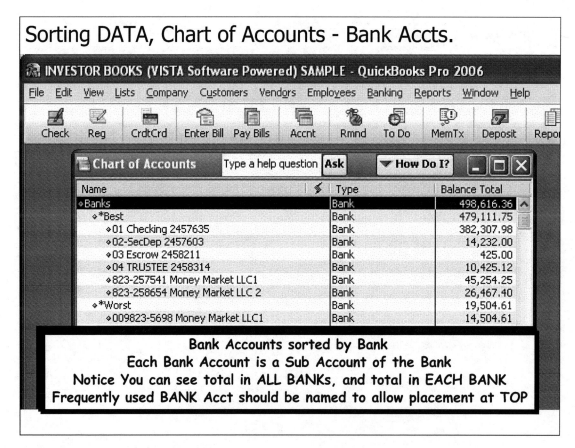

Sorting DATA, Chart of Accounts - Bank Accts.

INVESTOR BOOKS (VISTA Software Powered) SAMPLE - QuickBooks Pro 2006

File Edit View Lists Company Customers Vendors Employees Banking Reports Window Help

Check   Reg   CrdtCrd   Enter Bill Pay Bills   Accnt   Rmnd   To Do   MemTx   Deposit   Repor

Chart of Accounts   Type a help question Ask   ▼ How Do I?

Name	💲	Type	Balance Total
◇ Banks		Bank	498,616.36
◇ *Best		Bank	479,111.75
◇ 01 Checking 2457635		Bank	382,307.98
◇ 02-SecDep 2457603		Bank	14,232.00
◇ 03 Escrow 2458211		Bank	425.00
◇ 04 TRUSTEE 2458314		Bank	10,425.12
◇ 823-257541 Money Market LLC1		Bank	45,254.25
◇ 823-258654 Money Market LLC 2		Bank	26,467.40
◇ *Worst		Bank	19,504.61
◇ 009823-5698 Money Market LLC1		Bank	14,504.61

Bank Accounts sorted by Bank
Each Bank Account is a Sub Account of the Bank
Notice You can see total in ALL BANKs, and total in EACH BANK
Frequently used BANK Acct should be named to allow placement at TOP

In the next few screens, let's review briefly how the Chart of Accounts (Assets, Liabilities, Income, and Expenses) are set up using this system of naming accounts to benefit YOU.

Do not really worry about how to set it up. I want you to see how powerful this method becomes when you see it in action.

At the end of this brief review, you will see how easy and simple it becomes.

Bank accounts are asset accounts

      Each Bank will be a sub-account of your BANKS.

            Each Bank account will be a sub-account of each bank.

            This allows you to see how much

                $$$ in each bank account

                $$$ total in each bank

                $$$ total in ALL BANKS

Banks identify bank accounts by account numbers. USE ACCOUNT Numbers, the banks do.

Your most frequently used bank accounts, the one you use to write all the checks, etc, -- simply place a 01 in front to make it go to the top of your list.

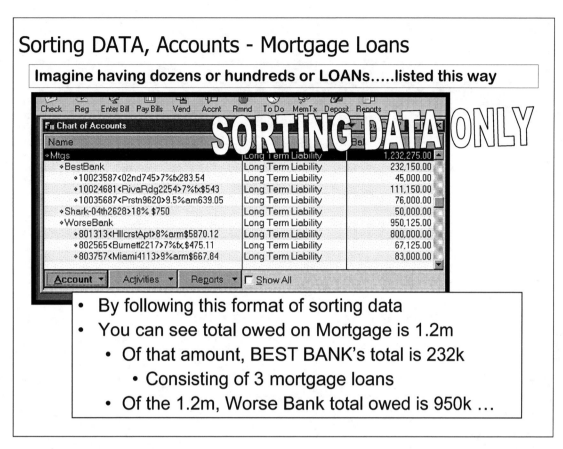

Sorting DATA, Accounts - Mortgage Loans

Imagine having dozens or hundreds or LOANs.....listed this way

- By following this format of sorting data
- You can see total owed on Mortgage is 1.2m
  - Of that amount, BEST BANK's total is 232k
    - Consisting of 3 mortgage loans
  - Of the 1.2m, Worse Bank total owed is 950k ...

Mortgages and Loans

Just like Banks, you will make each Lender a sub-account of MTGS (mortgages)

Each Mortgage or loan will be a sub-account of each lender.

This will allow you to see the balance owed on each loan, total owed to each lender, and total owed to ALL LENDERS.

Again, Lenders and Banks identify loans by account numbers and not by properties.

Investors identify and associate these loans by property.

How many times have you received correspondence from a lender about loan number 00825463 and you have no clue what property is involved. Let's make their system work to our advantage.

Loans will be named using this format

LoanNumber<Property><Rate,$Payment>

MASTER THIS GROUND RULE

STOP

Do **NOT** move forward
until understood 100%

Data entered WRONG
will be sorted WRONG....

You must MASTER this Ground Rule of Sorting Data.

If this subject is still FUZZY...

Go back and repeat it now...

Believe it or not, this is actually the hardest part.

If you do not understand what we just covered, everything will seem foreign.

It is all built on the foundation just shown in the previous

screens.

Use this account	To track
Bank	Checking, savings, and money market accounts. Add one bank account for every account your company has at a bank or other financial institution. (You can also use this type for petty cash.)
Accounts receivable (A/R)	Transactions related to the customers that owe you money, including invoices, payments, deposits of payments, refunds, credit memos, and statements. Most companies have only one A/R account.
Other current asset	Assets that are likely to be converted to cash or used up within one year, such as petty cash, notes receivable due within a year, prepaid expenses, and security deposits.
Fixed asset	Depreciable assets your company owns that aren't likely to be converted into cash within a year, such as equipment or furniture.
Other asset	Any asset that is neither a current asset nor a fixed asset, such as long-term notes receivable.
Accounts payable (A/P)	Transactions related to money you owe, including bills, bill payments, and any credit you have with vendors. See also current and long-term liability accounts.
Credit card	Credit card purchases, bills, and payments.
Current liability	Liabilities that are scheduled to be paid within one year, such as sales tax, payroll taxes, accrued or deferred salaries, and short-term loans.
Long-term liability	Liabilities such as loans or mortgages scheduled to be paid over periods longer than one year.
Equity	Owner's equity, including capital investment, drawings, and retained earnings.

Each of these 4 BASIC type of Accounts have additional weird sub-accounts.

I do not have these memorized and I do not expect to memorize them. The above Screenshot is taken directly from the HELP section of Quickbooks.

This powerful tool will assist you in determining what kind of account to utilize.

For example, if you were to loan a person $10,000 for 6 months, simply use the chart above to determine what kind of asset account to create for this transaction.

Types of QuickBooks accounts

account in the chart of accounts and click QuickReport.

Use this account	To track
Income	The main source of money coming into your company.
Other income	Money received for something other than normal business operations, such as interest income.
Expense	Money that's leaving your company.
Other expense	Money spent on something other than normal business operations, such as corporate taxes.
Cost of Goods sold	The cost of goods and materials held in inventory and then sold.

This is another view of the HELP section on different types of accounts.

This is so helpful, I included it in your manual.

A weird animal used later is the COGS or Cost of Goods Sold account. This is an expense account involved in selling real estate. It is used extensively later with closing statements involving the sale of property.

CAUTION:

COST OF GOODS SOLD

(COGS) is used ONLY AFTER you sell a property, NOT during fix up or getting ready....

SCHEDULE E (Form 1040)	Supplemental Income and Loss	OMB No. 1545-0074
Department of the Treasury Internal Revenue Service (99)	(From rental real estate, royalties, partnerships, S corporations, estates, trusts, REMICs, etc.) ► Attach to Form 1040 or Form 1041. ► See Instructions for Schedule E (Form 1040).	2001 Attachment Sequence No. 13

Name(s) shown on return | Your social security number

Part I Income or Loss From Rental Real Estate and Royalties Note. If you are in the business of renting personal property, use Schedule C or C-EZ (see page E-1). Report farm rental income or loss from **Form 4835** on page 2, line 39.

1 Show the kind and location of each **rental real estate property**:	2 For each rental real estate property listed on line 1, did you or your family use it during the tax year for personal purposes for more than the greater of: • 14 days **or** • 10% of the total days rented at fair rental value? (See page E-1.)	Yes	No
A	A		
B	B		
C	C		

		Properties			Totals (Add columns A, B, and C.)
Income:		A	B	C	
3 Rents received	3				3
4 Royalties received	4				4
Expenses:					
5 Advertising	5				
6 Auto and travel (see page E-2)	6				
7 Cleaning and maintenance	7				
8 Commissions	8				
9 Insurance	9				
10 Legal and other professional fees	10				
11 Management fees	11				
12 Mortgage interest paid to banks, etc. (see page E-2)	12				12
13 Other interest	13				

Use Schedule E, the IRS does

This is the IRS Schedule E.

Believe it or not, all of the extra income and expense accounts some folks use... and turn in to your tax preparer...you are paying them to condense your data and make it fit into this form.

USE SCHEDULE E, the IRS does.

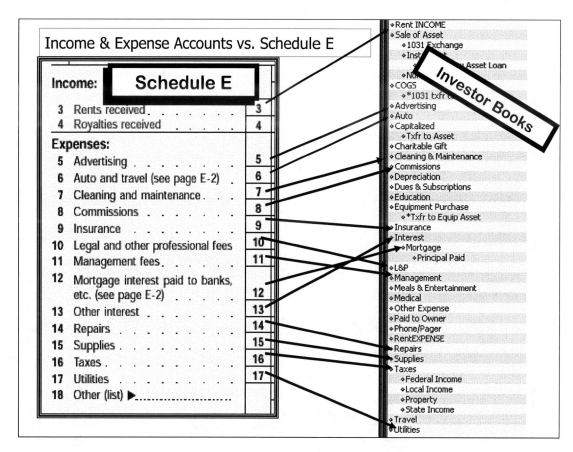

IRS Schedule E matched with Investor Books

On the Right are the Income and Expense Accounts already set up for you in Investor Books.

Everything on Schedule E can be found on the right.

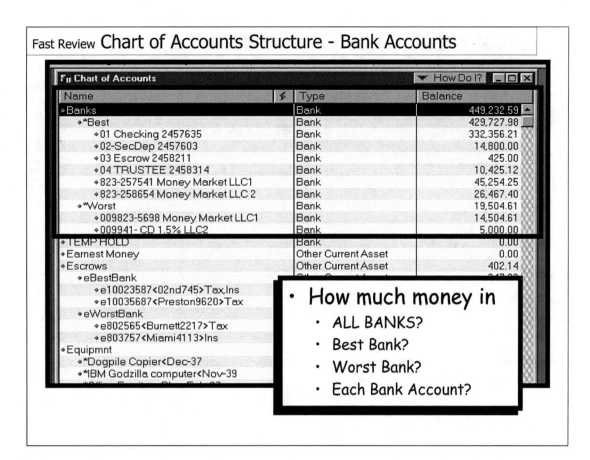

Do not start yet, let's do a quick review of the Chart of Accounts showing you the benefits of the naming accounts using these methods. Be patient.

This fast overview will show you how your Chart of Accounts are set up for you.

At the top, are your BANK ACCOUNTS

Chart of Accounts Structure - Escrows

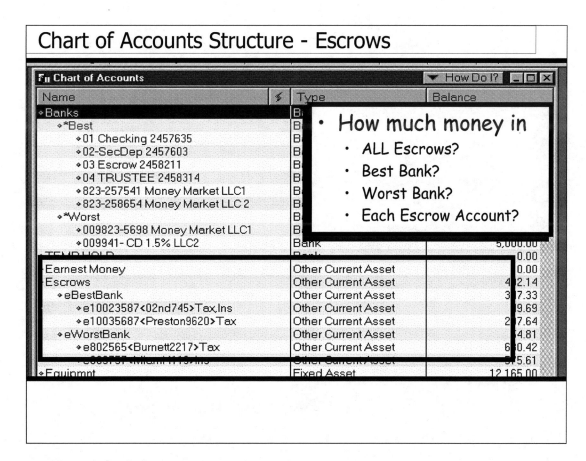

Followed by Escrow Accounts.

They are OTHER CURRENT ASSETs

Refer back to the screen of Quickbooks help and account definitions.

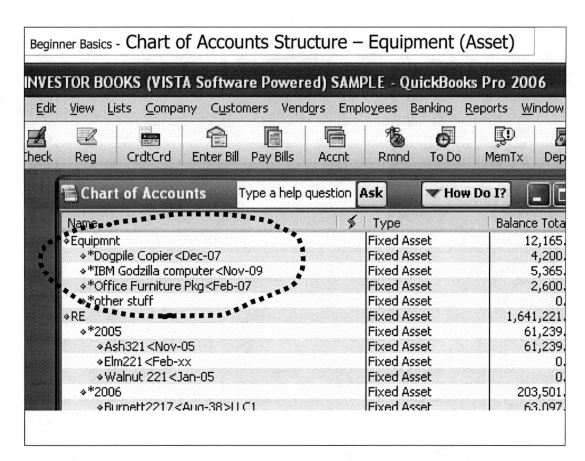

A small section of Fixed Assets listing EQUIPMENT OWNED.

Note the use of the * asterisk. This is a great way to prevent Quickbooks taking you to these seldom used accounts.

NOTE: Before making your decision to plug any equipment here, check with your tax advisor because you might be able to expense it all out this year! *(when you purchase any equipment, always use the Equip EXPENSE account)*

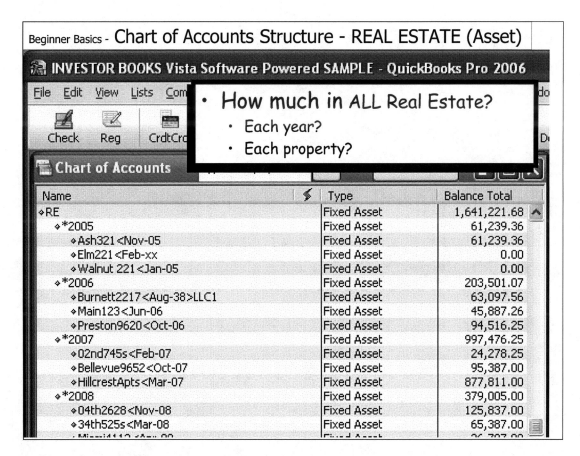

Beginner Basics - Chart of Accounts Structure - REAL ESTATE (Asset)

INVESTOR BOOKS Vista Software Powered SAMPLE - QuickBooks Pro 2006

File   Edit   View   Lists   Com

Check   Reg   CrdtCr

- **How much in ALL Real Estate?**
  - Each year?
  - Each property?

Chart of Accounts

Name	⚡	Type	Balance Total
◇RE		Fixed Asset	1,641,221.68
◇*2005		Fixed Asset	61,239.36
◇Ash321<Nov-05		Fixed Asset	61,239.36
◇Elm221<Feb-xx		Fixed Asset	0.00
◇Walnut 221<Jan-05		Fixed Asset	0.00
◇*2006		Fixed Asset	203,501.07
◇Burnett2217<Aug-38>LLC1		Fixed Asset	63,097.56
◇Main123<Jun-06		Fixed Asset	45,887.26
◇Preston9620<Oct-06		Fixed Asset	94,516.25
◇*2007		Fixed Asset	997,476.25
◇02nd745s<Feb-07		Fixed Asset	24,278.25
◇Bellevue9652<Oct-07		Fixed Asset	95,387.00
◇HillcrestApts<Mar-07		Fixed Asset	877,811.00
◇*2008		Fixed Asset	379,005.00
◇04th2628<Nov-08		Fixed Asset	125,837.00
◇34th525s<Mar-08		Fixed Asset	65,387.00
◇Miami4112<Aug-08		Fixed Asset	26,707.00

Followed by Real Estate owned.

Notice again, the *asterisk in front of the year.

*This prevents Quickbooks from taking you to the year. Odds are you could probably have a loan account number that could begin with 2005... or 2006545, if this were true, and you did not have an *asterisk in front of the year, Quickbooks would take you to the year instead of the loan, because the year appeared first.*

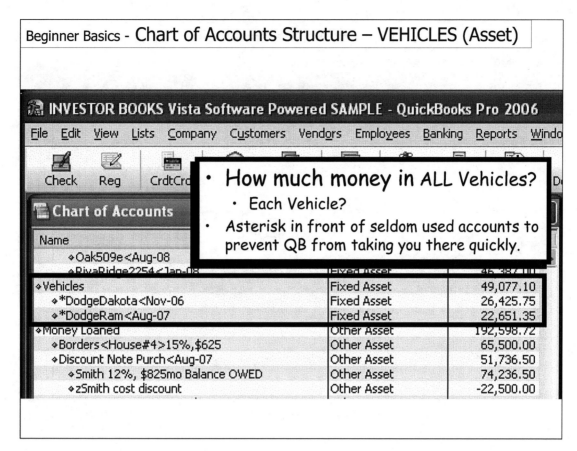

If your Real Estate operation own vehicles?

Even if you are a sole proprietorship you should list vehicles purchased and track real expenses associated with those vehicles.

Again, note the *asterisk in front of Dodge. Use the asterisk on accounts you would seldom look up. You can scroll down to find your Dodge vehicle(s).

Vehicles	*Fixed Asset*	*45,077.70*
◆*DodgeDakota<Nov-39	Fixed Asset	26,425.75
DodgeRam<Aug-39	*Fixed Asset*	*22,051.95*
◆Money Loaned	Other Asset	169,521.69
◆Borders<House#4>15%,$625	Other Asset	65,500.00
◆Grinnan<House18>15%,$825	Other Asset	75,362.22
◆Smith<House8>5%,$245	Other Asset	28,659.47
Accounts Payable	*Accounts Payable*	*0.00*
◆CrCds	Credit Card	0.00
◆*LLC1	Credit Card	0.00
◆AE 6655	Credit Card	0.00
◆MC 1141	Credit Card	0.00
◆Visa 5424	Credit Card	0.00

- ## How much money loaned?
  - ### Each Borrower?

10023307<JEnd7-197>6fx£03.31	*Long Term Liability*	*45,000.00*
◆10024681<RivaRdg2254>7%fx$543	Long Term Liability	111,150.00
◆10035687<Prstn9620>9.5%am639.05	Long Term Liability	76,000.00
◆Shark-04th2628>18% $750	Long Term Liability	50,000.00
◆WorseBank	Long Term Liability	950,125.00
◆801313<HllcrstApt>8%arm$5870.12	Long Term Liability	800,000.00
◆802565<Burnett2217>7%fx,$475.11	Long Term Liability	67,125.00

One of my favorites. Loaning money to other investors.

This is an **OTHER ASSET** account.

Make each loan as a "sub-account" to the **Money Loaned account.**

I think of borrowers by last name, not by account numbers like banks do; therefore, I name these accounts by the borrower last name, property secured, rate, payment.

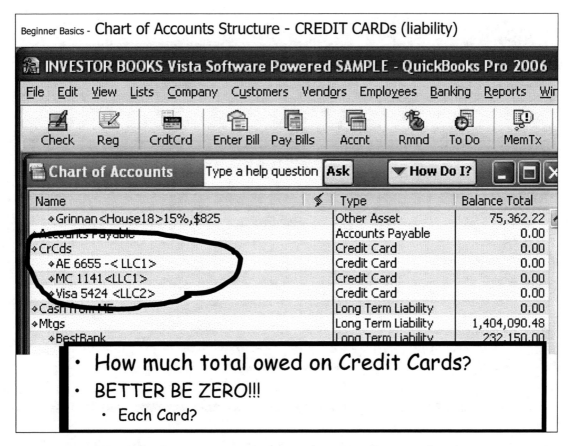

CREDIT CARDS... this is a very powerful and important feature of Quickbooks.

THE CREDIT CARD FEATURE can save you money!

• How many times have you bought gasoline and paid cash? – Do you get receipts and save them

• Have you ever eaten breakfast, lunch, or dinner, paid cash and lost the receipt?

• Have you ran to the hardware store to pick up last minute supplies, paid cash and lost receipts?

STOP IT NOW! Use a Credit Card and it will create a back up system of documentation for you by creating an additional receipt.

All GAS, meals, supplies, EVERYTHING... put it on the card, and you can get Skymiles too if you are lucky.

With multiple entities, such as LLCs, look at how you simply add an abbreviation identifier to the end of the account name.

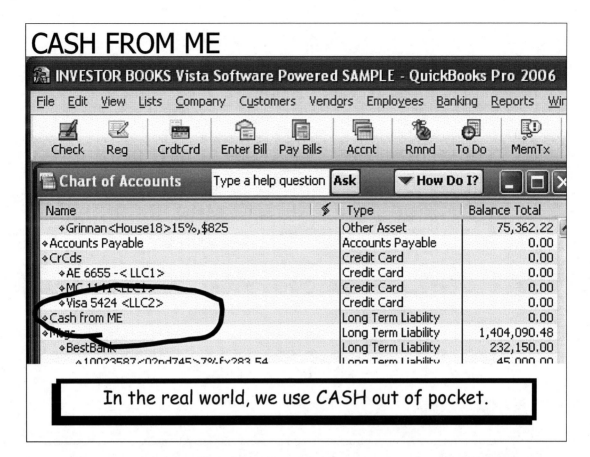

In the real world, we use CASH out of pocket.

CASH FROM ME account is HUGE!

Here's the deal. Suppose you "loan your real estate operation" $5,000 from your personal bank account…. Hmmm, how do I enter it?

Step 1. – Click on the DEPOSIT Speed Button. Enter the proper date, and dollar amount, and in the ACCOUNT Field, enter "CASH FROM ME"

When you push the record button, Investor Books just INCREASED your CASH FROM ME account to $5,000 and increased your bank account balance by $5,000… (It the old post office thing, just pulling 5k from a liability wall account and depositing it into an Asset Wall account, your bank account)

You can also use the CASH FROM ME account for real world stuff like stopping by Home Depot and buying stuff and paying cash. Hang on to your receipt. When you get home, OPEN the CASH FROM ME Register and enter date, paid to Home Depot, $36.00 for repairs (faucet) for house #12… now it will show your real estate operation OWES You the $36.00 for the purchase you made.

Chart of Accounts – MORTGAGES (liability)

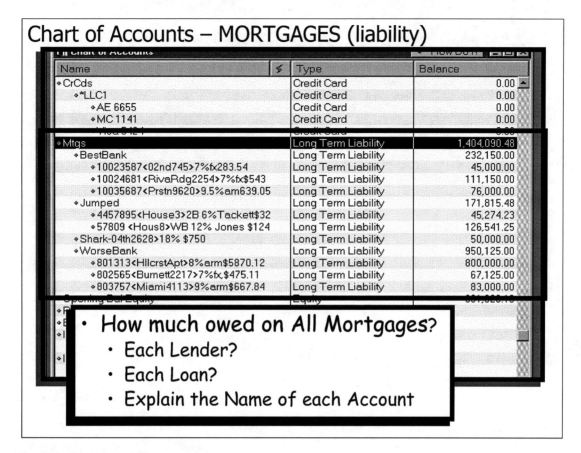

Name	⚡	Type	Balance
◆ CrCds		Credit Card	0.00
◆ *LLC1		Credit Card	0.00
◆ AE 6655		Credit Card	0.00
◆ MC 1141		Credit Card	0.00
◆ Mtgs		Long Term Liability	1,404,090.48
◆ BestBank		Long Term Liability	232,150.00
◆ 10023587<02nd745>7%fx283.54		Long Term Liability	45,000.00
◆ 10024681<RivaRdg2254>7%fx$543		Long Term Liability	111,150.00
◆ 10035687<Prstn9620>9.5%am639.05		Long Term Liability	76,000.00
◆ Jumped		Long Term Liability	171,815.48
◆ 4457895<House3>2B 6%Tackett$32		Long Term Liability	45,274.23
◆ 57809 <Hous8>WB 12% Jones $124		Long Term Liability	126,541.25
◆ Shark-04th2628>18% $750		Long Term Liability	50,000.00
◆ WorseBank		Long Term Liability	950,125.00
◆ 801313<HllcrstApt>8%arm$5870.12		Long Term Liability	800,000.00
◆ 802565<Burnett2217>7%fx.$475.11		Long Term Liability	67,125.00
◆ 803757<Miami4113>9%arm$667.84		Long Term Liability	83,000.00

- **How much owed on All Mortgages?**
  - Each Lender?
  - Each Loan?
  - Explain the Name of each Account

Mortgages – as noted earlier,

Lenders are sub accounts of MTGS.

     - loans are sub-accounts of each lender

Pay Special attention to the proper way to name each loan account.

STUDY this one for a moment,

DO NOT FLIP THIS PAGE FAST

TIP: If you have Bank Accounts with some of the same lenders, place an *asterisk on the BANK Names at the top of your Chart of Accounts. Do NOT place an *asterisk in front of Lender name here. It is very far down the list. In this example, you could simply enter BestBank and Quickbooks would take you straight to the mortgages of Best Bank.

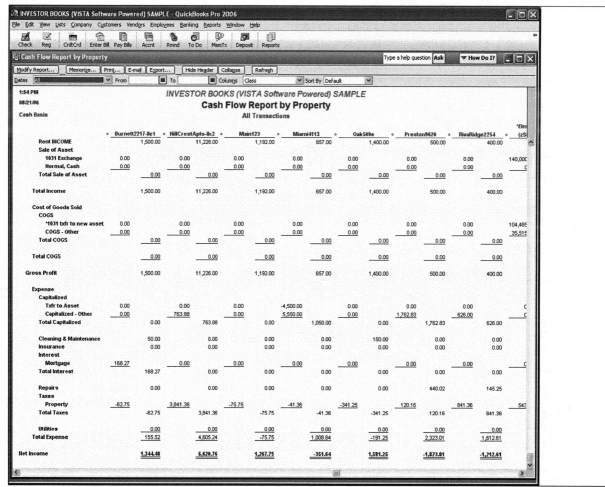

Study this Profit and Loss Report

This is used for end of year for taxes.

Notice Capitalized Expenses have been ZERO'd out for tax purposes, but the investor can still see how much CA$H was spent.

Mortgage Interest and principal speaks for itself.

Each column represents a property and notice total for LLC and Total for All.

All contained on one page. If you had 30 properties, you would have a number of pages and still have each property's performance displayed in a single column on ONE PAGE. This is why you want to keep income and expense accounts to a minimum.

Before getting into Income and Expense accounts, **you need to see the benefit first.**

Here's a Profit and Loss Report using Income and Expense Accounts..

Hopefully you can appreciate the structure of the Income and Expense Accounts with this report.

Remember, Post Office Boxes with same kind of Income and Expense accounts?

Now it should be coming together.

(L&P) is Legal and Professional (I had someone ask me this question and chose to include it here)

The easiest way to explain Income & Expense Accounts

Let's Start at the end with an actual Report.

Here is a PROFIT & LOSS

NOTICE how all Income & Expense Accounts fit into one column on the left.

Accounts not used will not be displayed.

This allows for each column to represent a Property.

If you had a boatload of Accounts, = 2+ Page Report, UGLY

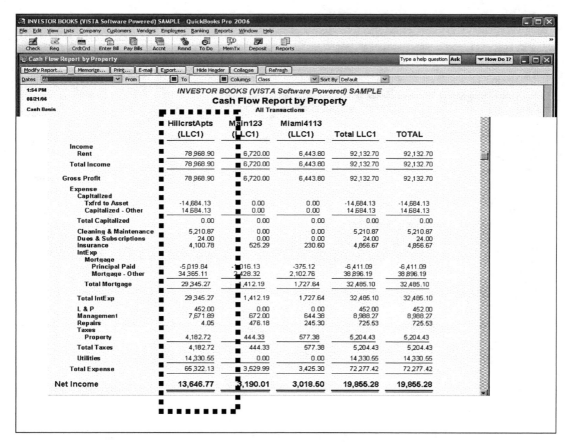

Study this Profit and Loss Report

This is used for end of year for taxes.

Notice Capitalized Expenses have been ZERO'd out for tax purposes, but the investor can still see how much CA$H was spent.

Mortgage Interest and principal speaks for itself.

Each column represents a property and notice total for LLC and Total for All.

All contained on one page. If you had 30 properties, you would have a number of pages and still have each property's performance displayed in a single column on ONE PAGE. This is why you want to keep income and expense accounts to a minimum.

The big bold red dotted highlighted area shows the income and expenses for a particular property.

Just like the post office, each column represents a property.

(Imagine having 40 or more income and expense accounts. What a nightmare, this would cause you to have TWO PAGES to see the bottom line on each property... ugly. NEVER add income or expense accounts. You should only add properties, bank accounts, loans, and entities)

KEEP IT SHORT and to one page. You want each property to be displayed in a column to be viewed on one page. If you have 200 properties, each page could display the performance of 5 or more properties. I actually use the "landscape" paper layout and get about 8 or 10 properties to each page.

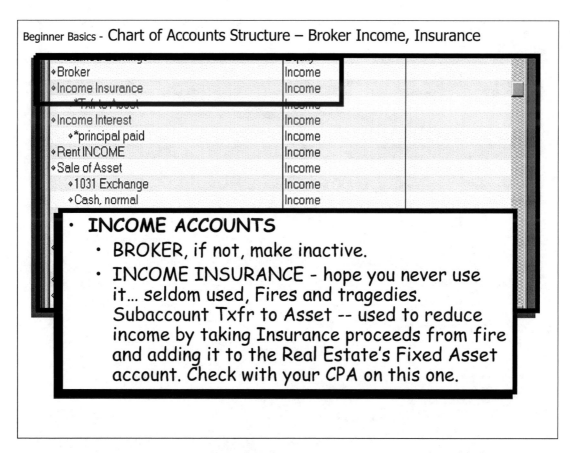

◆Broker	Income	
◆Income Insurance	Income	
*Txfr to Asset	Income	
◆Income Interest	Income	
◆*principal paid	Income	
◆Rent INCOME	Income	
◆Sale of Asset	Income	
◆1031 Exchange	Income	
◆Cash, normal	Income	

- **INCOME ACCOUNTS**
  - BROKER, if not, make inactive.
  - INCOME INSURANCE - hope you never use it... seldom used, Fires and tragedies. Subaccount Txfr to Asset -- used to reduce income by taking Insurance proceeds from fire and adding it to the Real Estate's Fixed Asset account. Check with your CPA on this one.

If you feel some do not pertain to you, simply make them inactive and hold for future use.

MAKE THEM INACTIVE, Do NOT Delete them.

The BROKER income is example. If you are a broker, keep it, if not, make inactive.

INCOME INSURANCE, seldom used, but you may get checks for things like fires, hail damage, tornadoes, etc. When this happens, check with the real estate tax expert, you may be able to defer this income.

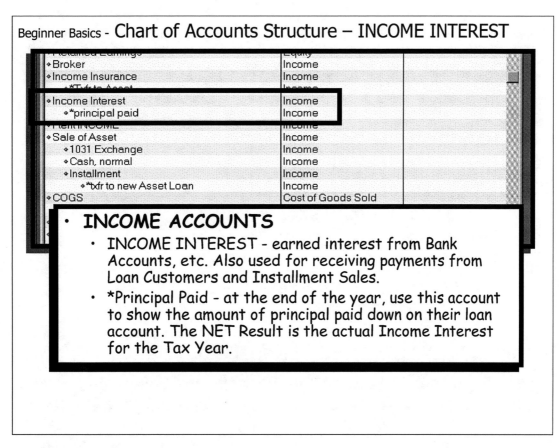

◆Broker	Income	
◆Income Insurance	Income	
◆*Txfr to Asset	Income	
◆Income Interest	Income	
◆*principal paid	Income	
◆Rent INCOME	Income	
◆Sale of Asset	Income	
◆1031 Exchange	Income	
◆Cash, normal	Income	
◆Installment	Income	
◆*txfr to new Asset Loan	Income	
◆COGS	Cost of Goods Sold	

- **INCOME ACCOUNTS**
  - INCOME INTEREST - earned interest from Bank Accounts, etc. Also used for receiving payments from Loan Customers and Installment Sales.
  - *Principal Paid - at the end of the year, use this account to show the amount of principal paid down on their loan account. The NET Result is the actual Income Interest for the Tax Year.

INCOME INTEREST is not to be confused with Interest:Mortgage.

Many bank accounts actually do pay interest on funds held. Money market accounts, CDs, savings, etc. along with loans you make to borrowers.

When YOU loan money, ALL of your loan customer's payment is dumped into your Income Interest account and you will settle it up once a year for tax reporting purposes.

Unfortunately, loan customers, just like tenants do silly things like bouncing checks. Do not waste your time with trying to separate principal, interest, and late charges.

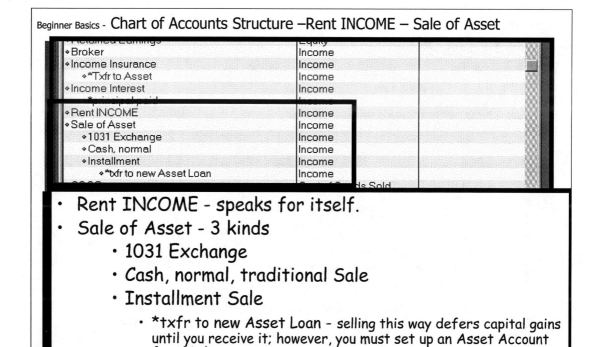

◆ Broker	Income
◆ Income Insurance	Income
◆ *Txfr to Asset	Income
◆ Income Interest	Income
◆ Rent INCOME	Income
◆ Sale of Asset	Income
◆ 1031 Exchange	Income
◆ Cash, normal	Income
◆ Installment	Income
◆ *txfr to new Asset Loan	Income

- Rent INCOME - speaks for itself.
- Sale of Asset - 3 kinds
  - 1031 Exchange
  - Cash, normal, traditional Sale
  - Installment Sale
    - *txfr to new Asset Loan - selling this way defers capital gains until you receive it; however, you must set up an Asset Account for this loan customer.

You'll see more when entering Installment Sale Transaction

RENT INCOME is one of my favorites.

SALE OF ASSET is another payday income account.

For TAX PURPOSES, there are
ONLY 3 ways to sell property PERIOD.

Much more detail on this later with closing statements.

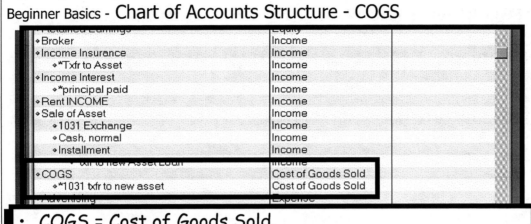

Broker	Income
Income Insurance	Income
*Txfr to Asset	Income
Income Interest	Income
*principal paid	Income
Rent INCOME	Income
Sale of Asset	Income
1031 Exchange	Income
Cash, normal	Income
Installment	Income
txfr to new Asset Loan	Income
COGS	Cost of Goods Sold
*1031 txfr to new asset	Cost of Goods Sold
Advertising	Expense

- COGS = Cost of Goods Sold.
- KISS METHOD --
  - Cash Sale Price of House = 50k
    - *Fixed Asset had 30k, reduced to ZERO using COGS*
  - Profit & Loss now shows 20k profit
  - Fixed Asset Account for House shows ZERO Balance.
    ## You can NOT sell it and still own it.

COGS = Cost of Goods SOLD. Another good feature of Quickbooks.

Use ONLY AFTER You've SOLD a property, **NEVER** during rehab

It does NOT say use on properties you intend to sell... it says SOLD.

The above SALE OF ASSET income account and the sub-accounts get only one entry.. IF you have ever sold a property, odds are you probably signed an IRS Form 1099 listing the SALE PRICE of your property as income. You always want the SALE PRICE ONLY to be entered into the SALE OF ASSET income account.

All of the expenses involved in selling your investment are entered into the COGS expense account, thus reducing the income from Sale of Asset to show your gross profit.

Chart of Accounts Structure - INCOME & EXPENSE

Expense				
Capitalized				
Txfr to Asset	0.00		0.00	0.00
Capitalized - Other	0.00		763.88	0.00
Total Capitalized		0.00	763.88	
Cleaning & Maintenance		50.00	0.00	
Insurance		0.00	0.00	
Interest				
Mortgage	168.27		0.00	0.00
Total Interest		168.27	0.00	
Repairs		0.00	0.00	
Taxes				
Property	-62.75		3,841.36	-75.75
Total Taxes		-62.75	3,841.36	
Utilities		0.00	0.00	
Total Expense		155.52	4,605.24	
Net Income		**1,344.48**	**6,620.76**	

Remember earlier we talked about accountants and bookkeepers creating reports that are worthless to investors.

If you are one these people, pay close attention on this one.

Notice the first row circled is a **Capitalized Expense** account. Your accountant has been trained to not put these things on a profit and loss report.

For example, the investor buys a house, fixes it up, and rents it out. No problem.. yet... let's say 2 years later, the investor puts a $4,200 roof on this rental property. If he has a good accountant who produces a report, the $4,200 roof expense does NOT show up on the investor profit and loss report. The investor gets frustrated and pissed off because he KNOWS he wrote a check to the roofer for $4,200 and it came out of the bank account.. No fantasy there... but yet the accountant starts spilling all of this bean counting lingo about the proper this and the proper that...end result, the investor shakes his head, tells the accountant the report is absolutely worthless and both are baffled. Investor feels he is wasting money on an accountant and the accountant is confused because they believe they are doing it properly and the investor fails to understand.

Back to the report. From now on, you will enter Capitalized items into the **CAPITALIZED EXPENSE** account.

Notice there is a sub account called Transferred to Asset. At the end of the year, you use this account to transfer the amount of Capitalized Expenses to the Fixed Asset Account associated with the expense. (Look at the top of the column, it will identify the property involved.)

Capitalized Expenses get transferred to the Fixed Asset account, and they are depreciated over the life of the item, BUT the investor can still see how much CASH was actually spent on those Capitalized Expenses.

Chart of Accounts Structure - INCOME & EXPENSE

Expense			
Capitalized			
Txfr to Asset	0.00	0.00	0.00
Capitalized - Other	0.00	763.88	0.00
Total Capitalized	0.00	763.88	
Cleaning & Maintenance	50.00	0.00	
Insurance	0.00	0.00	
Interest			
Mortgage	168.27	0.00	0.00
Total Interest	168.27	0.00	
Repairs	0.00	0.00	
Taxes			
Property	-62.75	3,841.36	-75.75
Total Taxes	-62.75	3,841.36	
Utilities	0.00	0.00	
Total Expense	155.52	4,605.24	
Net Income	**1,344.48**	**6,620.76**	

Interest and Mortgage Interest are structured in a very similar way.

Unfortunately, Quickbooks does not amortize loans.

DO NOT BREAK DOWN THE MONTHLY PRINCIPAL AND INTEREST.. If you want to do this every month, you have too much time on your hands.

This is accomplished properly by dumping all of the principal and interest loan payment into the mortgage interest expense account. At the end of the year, you use the principal paid sub account to enter the amount of principal reduction into the specific liability "mortgage loan account"

Now, you can see how much CASH you are out for mortgage payments, and how much mortgage interest expense for the year along with how much principal paid down for each property and TOTALS FOR THE YEAR

STEP 2, enter principal paid down on each mortgage loan using the Principal Paid subaccount of Mortgage Interest.

Now you can see how much you paid in Mortgage Interest

Don't worry about how to do it right now, this screen intends to show you how to understand the appearance of this report.

ALSO NOTICE far right column, total principal paid down for all properties, total interest paid, etc, etc.

POWERFUL BUSINESS INFORMATION

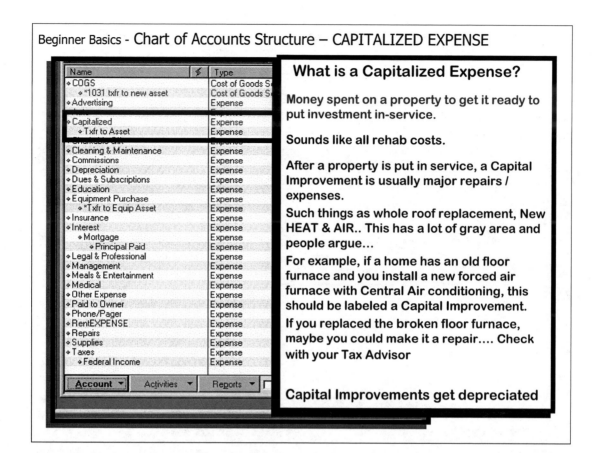

Name	$	Type
◆ COGS		Cost of Goods S
◆ *1031 txfr to new asset		Cost of Goods S
◆ Advertising		Expense
		Expense
◆ Capitalized		Expense
◆ Txfr to Asset		Expense
◆ Cleaning & Maintenance		Expense
◆ Commissions		Expense
◆ Depreciation		Expense
◆ Dues & Subscriptions		Expense
◆ Education		Expense
◆ Equipment Purchase		Expense
◆ *Txfr to Equip Asset		Expense
◆ Insurance		Expense
◆ Interest		Expense
◆ Mortgage		Expense
◆ Principal Paid		Expense
◆ Legal & Professional		Expense
◆ Management		Expense
◆ Meals & Entertainment		Expense
◆ Medical		Expense
◆ Other Expense		Expense
◆ Paid to Owner		Expense
◆ Phone/Pager		Expense
◆ RentEXPENSE		Expense
◆ Repairs		Expense
◆ Supplies		Expense
◆ Taxes		Expense
◆ Federal Income		Expense

[Account ▼] [Activities ▼] [Reports ▼]

What is a Capitalized Expense?

Money spent on a property to get it ready to put investment in-service.

Sounds like all rehab costs.

After a property is put in service, a Capital Improvement is usually major repairs / expenses.

Such things as whole roof replacement, New HEAT & AIR.. This has a lot of gray area and people argue...

For example, if a home has an old floor furnace and you install a new forced air furnace with Central Air conditioning, this should be labeled a Capital Improvement.

If you replaced the broken floor furnace, maybe you could make it a repair.... Check with your Tax Advisor

Capital Improvements get depreciated

Capitalized Expense

Notice the sub account called Transferred to Asset. At the end of the year, this account is used to transfer the amount of Capitalized Expenses to the Fixed Asset Account (Look at the top of the column, it will identify the property involved.)

These are depreciated over the life of the item, BUT the investor can still see how much CASH was actually spent on those Capitalized Expenses.

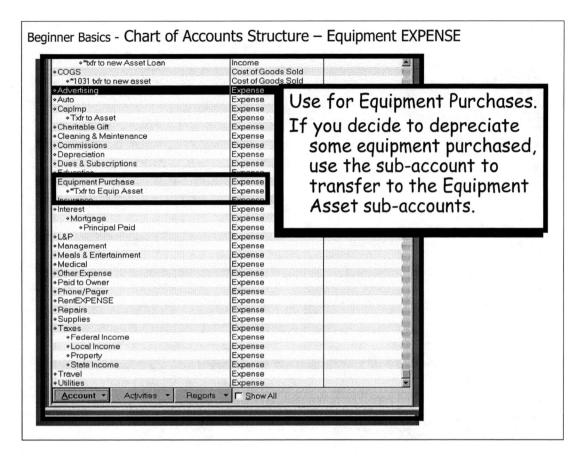

Beginner Basics - Chart of Accounts Structure – Equipment EXPENSE

◦ *txfr to new Asset Loan	Income
◦ COGS	Cost of Goods Sold
◦ *1031 txfr to new asset	Cost of Goods Sold
◦ Advertising	Expense
◦ Auto	Expense
◦ CapImp	Expense
◦ Txfr to Asset	Expense
◦ Charitable Gift	Expense
◦ Cleaning & Maintenance	Expense
◦ Commissions	Expense
◦ Depreciation	Expense
◦ Dues & Subscriptions	Expense
◦ Education	Expense
Equipment Purchase	Expense
◦ *Txfr to Equip Asset	Expense
◦ Insurance	Expense
◦ Interest	Expense
◦ Mortgage	Expense
◦ Principal Paid	Expense
◦ L&P	Expense
◦ Management	Expense
◦ Meals & Entertainment	Expense
◦ Medical	Expense
◦ Other Expense	Expense
◦ Paid to Owner	Expense
◦ Phone/Pager	Expense
◦ RentEXPENSE	Expense
◦ Repairs	Expense
◦ Supplies	Expense
◦ Taxes	Expense
◦ Federal Income	Expense
◦ Local Income	Expense
◦ Property	Expense
◦ State Income	Expense
◦ Travel	Expense
◦ Utilities	Expense

Account ▾   Activities ▾   Reports ▾   ☐ Show All

> **Use for Equipment Purchases.**
> If you decide to depreciate some equipment purchased, use the sub-account to transfer to the Equipment Asset sub-accounts.

Occasionally you will purchase equipment to assist with your real estate investments.

Use the Equipment Purchase Expense account.

Depending on the most recent tax law and the equipment purchased, you may choose to transfer this expense to an Equipment Asset account. Again, use the sub-account to transfer it to allow you to see the CA$H.

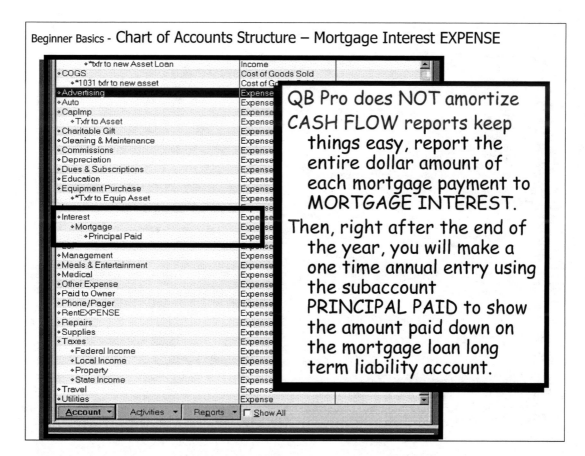

The inset screen shows a Chart of Accounts list with the following entries:

Account	Type
◆*txfr to new Asset Loan	Income
◆COGS	Cost of Goods Sold
◆*1031 txfr to new asset	Cost of G...
◆Advertising	Expense
◆Auto	Expense
◆CapImp	Expense
◆Txfr to Asset	Expense
◆Charitable Gift	Expense
◆Cleaning & Maintenance	Expense
◆Commissions	Expense
◆Depreciation	Expense
◆Dues & Subscriptions	Expense
◆Education	Expense
◆Equipment Purchase	Expense
◆*Txfr to Equip Asset	Expense
◆Interest	Expense
◆Mortgage	Expense
◆Principal Paid	Expense
◆Management	Expense
◆Meals & Entertainment	Expense
◆Medical	Expense
◆Other Expense	Expense
◆Paid to Owner	Expense
◆Phone/Pager	Expense
◆RentEXPENSE	Expense
◆Repairs	Expense
◆Supplies	Expense
◆Taxes	Expense
◆Federal Income	Expense
◆Local Income	Expense
◆Property	Expense
◆State Income	Expense
◆Travel	Expense
◆Utilities	Expense

Account ▼   Activities ▼   Reports ▼   ☐ Show All

Callout note:

QB Pro does NOT amortize

CASH FLOW reports keep things easy, report the entire dollar amount of each mortgage payment to MORTGAGE INTEREST.

Then, right after the end of the year, you will make a one time annual entry using the subaccount PRINCIPAL PAID to show the amount paid down on the mortgage loan long term liability account.

Mortgage Interest Expense Account.

As described earlier, this is a very important part of your cash flow tool allowing you to see total cash out of pocket to pay all loans and mortgage payments, how principal paid down at the end of the year, mortgage interest expense totals and totals for all for the year and can be compared in any manner you wish.

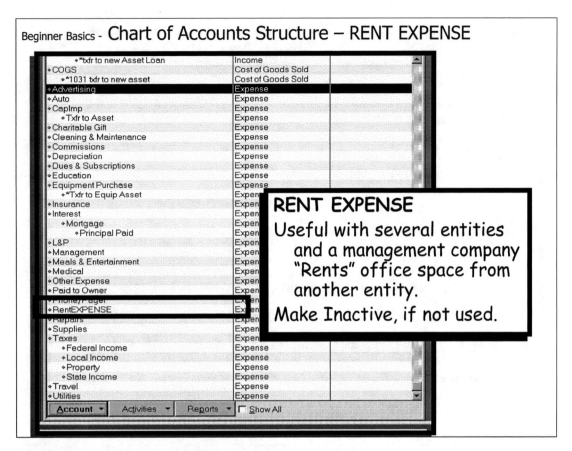

RENT EXPENSE
Useful with several entities
and a management company
"Rents" office space from
another entity.
Make Inactive, if not used.

RENT EXPENSE... if you have your management
company and your management company rents office space
and/or office equipment from some other entity you own, your
management company would be paying a RENT EXPENSE.

If you do not RENT Office space for example, MAKE THIS
INACTIVE.

Do NOT use this to rent a concrete saw or floor sander.

- EXAMPLE
- Bill from John Smith for $100 for Repairs to House #3 for hanging a new gutter.
- Prepare check to John Smith $100, Repairs to House #3.
- IN THE **MEMO** Field,
  - use 3-6 words
  - briefly describe the repair
  - example for the memo field may be "new gutter"

  NOW - does CPA need to call you?

Use the MEMO field
It will SAVE you money!

time, and trips to your file cabinets searching for receipts or more paperwork.

The above example describes a REPAIR expense paid to a person. Without a brief description of 3 or 4 words describing the repair, you would have no clue what the repair involves.

Start doing this NOW, it is a good habit.

Getting Started - first desktop view

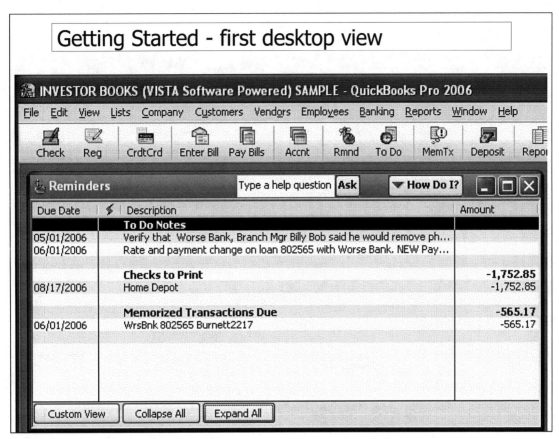

You'll see this every time you open Investor Books

Made a "back up" of file

NOW to get started.

We'll explain briefly what you are looking at on your desktop.

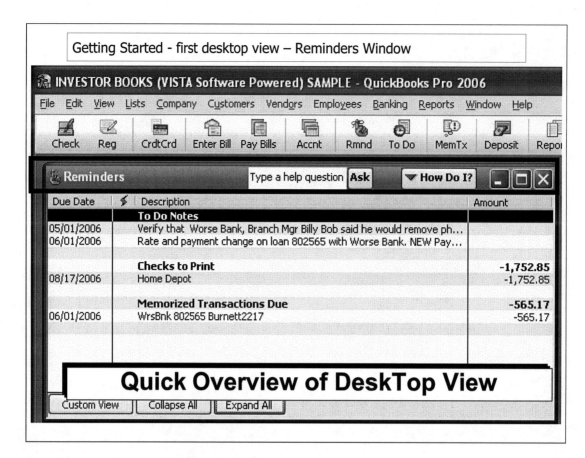

Getting Started - first desktop view – Reminders Window

Quick Overview of DeskTop View

Reminder Window

Opens every time you open your Investor Books made EZ file, powerful reminder tool

Displays "To Do's", checks to print, scheduled transactions, etc.

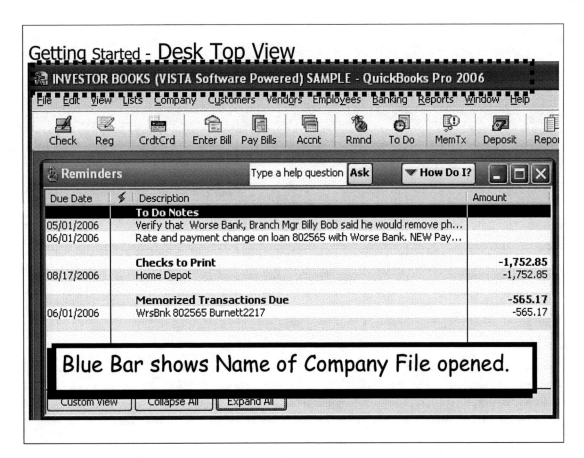

Getting Started - Desk Top View

The Blue Bar at the top displays the Quickbooks company file you have open.

It should be

INVESTOR BOOKS made EZ.

(If you have Tenant Tracking open, Tenant Tracking will be displayed here)

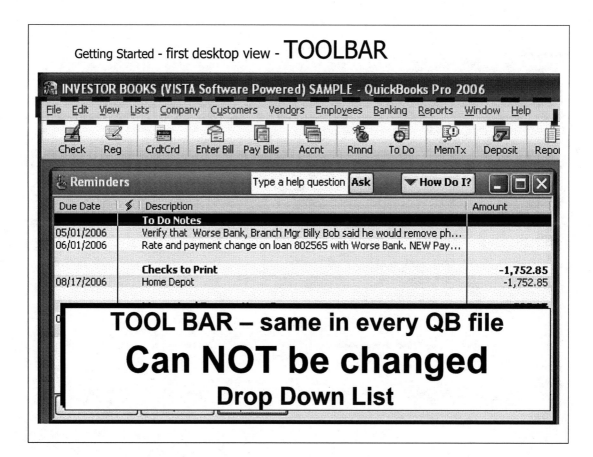

Getting Started - first desktop view - TOOLBAR

TOOL BAR – same in every QB file
Can NOT be changed
Drop Down List

This is the TOOL BAR

Each Name has a "Drop Down" list

Each Drop Down list contains activities related to the Tool Bar Name

Including powerful "HELP"

The TOOL BAR can not be changed and will appear exactly as displayed in any Quickbooks company file.

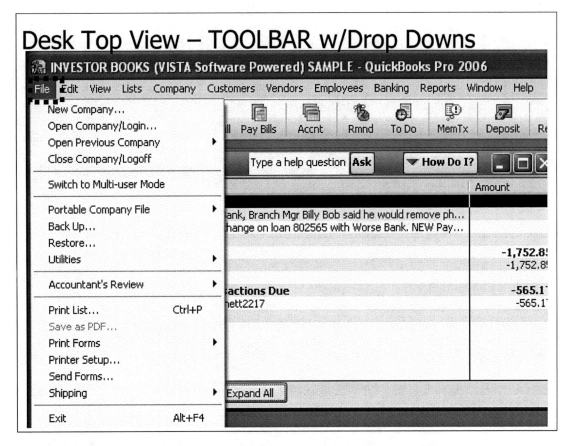

Desk Top View – TOOLBAR w/Drop Downs

Every name in the "Tool Bar" has a drop down list.

Displayed is an example of a drop down list from the word FILE.

Again, this is the same in ALL QB company files and can not be customized.

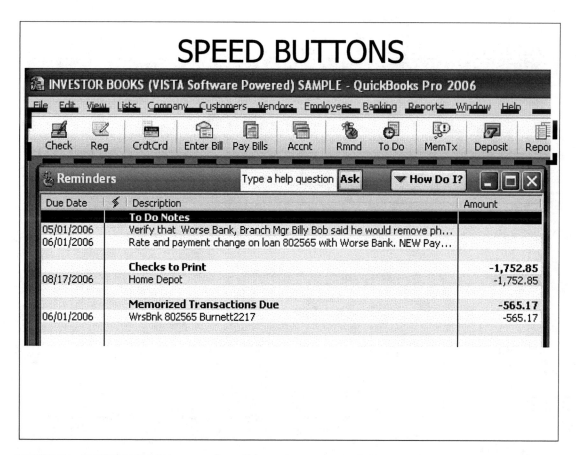

SPEED BUTTONS

SPEED BUTTONS can be found under the toolbar on your desktop view.

QB calls these ICONs and ICON BAR.

I don't know why, but years ago, QB called them Speed Buttons.

The most frequently used procedures and reports are already set up for you.

At this time, we will review each button one at a time and explain the function of each Speed Button.

After reviewing the function of each Speed Button, you will start setting up your properties.

SPEED BUTTON - create a CHECK

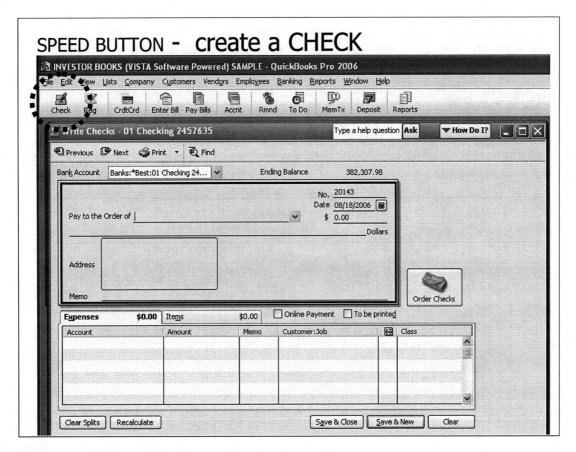

Used to CREATE A CHECK.

Clicking on the create CHECK speed button, opens the create check window.

You should set it up to default to the most frequently used bank account.

You can select another bank account right from this create check window.

SPEED BUTTON - Registers

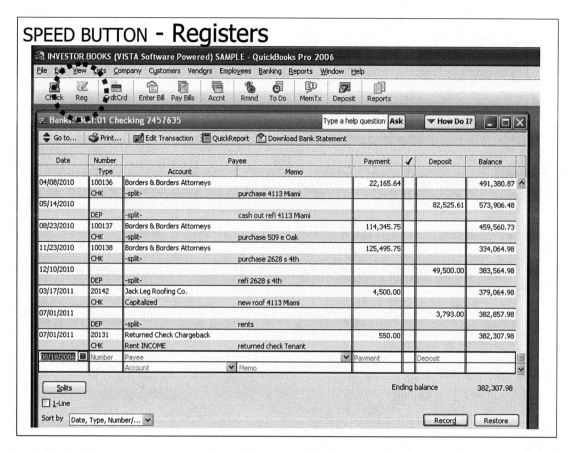

You have choose to have the register open automatically and this is the result.

Very user friendly.

Displays the date, Payee, amount, and balance of each transaction in chronological order.

If you have entered transactions in advance of today's date, a bright neon blue line highlights and separates future dated transactions. You will like this later.

NOTE: pay attention to the MEMO field, it describes briefly each transaction. It will help you.

SPEED BUTTON – Credit Cards including Personal Purchases

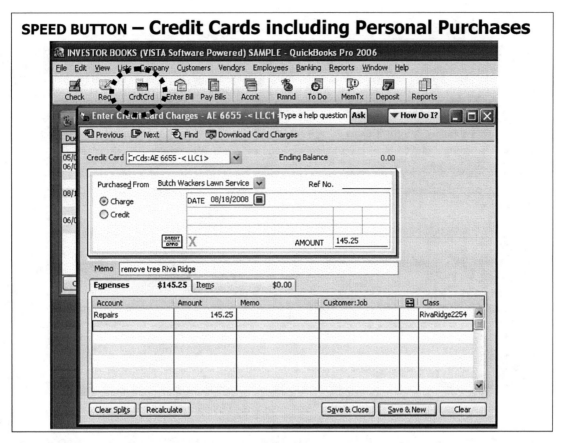

Even if you ignore your credit card until you receive your monthly bill, still enter all of your credit card charges using this feature. (This is exactly what I do today)

Do NOT pay the credit card bill with a check and a large split transaction. It will kill your reports on your vendors.

If you use credit cards, use the credit card feature and ENTER each transaction noted on your credit card statement.

It is powerful

Easy to follow, just tab through it.

We do not live in a perfect world.

Sometimes, we use our real estate credit card for PERSONAL PURCHASES.

EZ, no problem, Here is how to enter it properly.

1.) Enter the proper Vendor "Pay to ...."

2.) Enter the date of purchase, and amount

3.) Account Field, enter CASH FROM ME

4.) Enter dollar amount.

5.) MEMO field, describe it if you can remember it.

6.) CLASS, entity used for the purchase, whose bank account.

Chart of Accounts - CREDIT CARDs (liability)

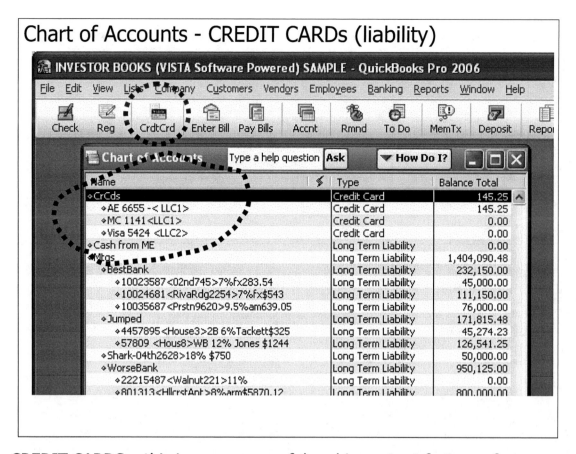

CREDIT CARDS... this is a very powerful and important feature of Quickbooks. USE IT

THE CREDIT CARD FEATURE in QB is Powerful and it can save you money! (try not carry balances on credit cards)

How many times have you bought gasoline and paid cash? – Do you get receipts and save them?

Have you ever eaten breakfast, lunch, or dinner, paid cash and lost the receipt?

Have you ran to the hardware store to pick up last minute supplies, paid cash and lost receipts?

STOP IT NOW! Use a Credit Card (but pay it off every month) and it will create a back up system of documentation for you by creating an additional receipt.

All GAS, meals, supplies, EVERYTHING... put it on the card, and you can get Skymiles too if you are lucky.

Speed Button - ENTER BILLS

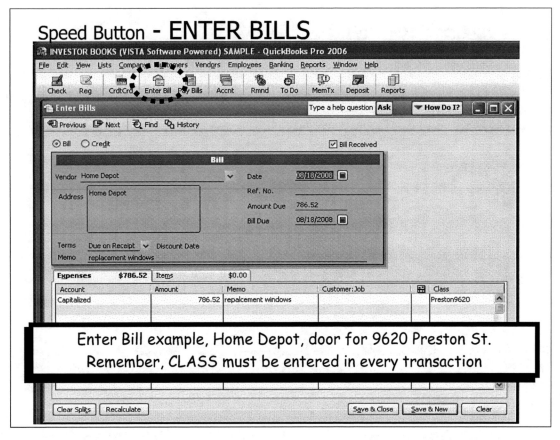

Enter Bill example, Home Depot, door for 9620 Preston St.
Remember, CLASS must be entered in every transaction

Displayed above is an example of a billed entered for Home Depot to be paid at a later date.

CLASS must be used on every transaction.

Use the MEMO field, it describes what was purchased, instead of just labeling the transaction a Repair for "something" purchased at Home Depot. You can see it was for panel doors.

A real world example of this... If you have a Home Depot Commercial account, or a Lowe's Business Account, or a paint store account, etc.

Speed Button PAY BILLS

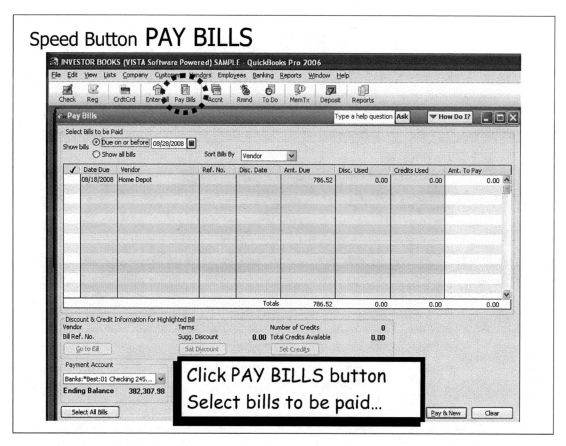

Click PAY BILLS button
Select bills to be paid...

Used when you receive a statement from a vendor who wants to be paid once a month.

Click on the PAY BILLS speed button displays outstanding or unpaid bills.

You can sort by Vendor, allowing only the unpaid bills for the selected vendor to be displayed.

Click on the bills you want to pay

A Good Example of this:

-Home Depot Commercial Account

- Lowe's Business Account

- Paint Store account

- Brokers use it for agent commissions, fees, and charges.

Speed Button **PAY BILLS**

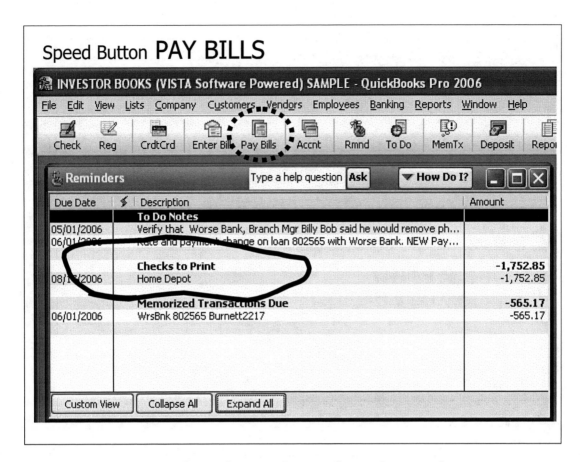

If you print checks, the check to be printed to the vendor just paid would now also be displayed in your reminders window.

Speed Button – VENDOR (before 2006)

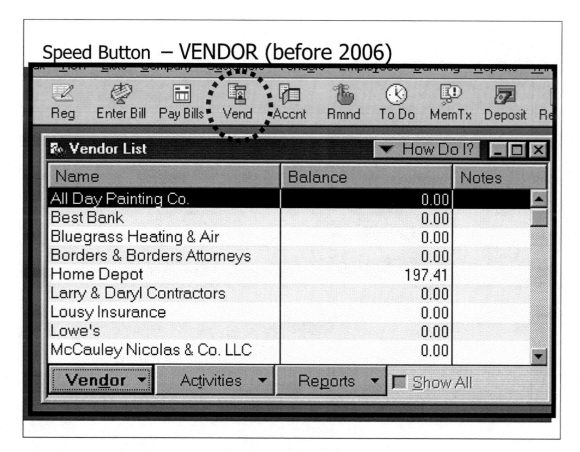

VENDOR speed button display the list.

Notice the balance column. In the displayed example, there is a outstanding balance of $197.41 owed to Home Depot for bills entered in the system.

Do NOT worry about building this list. Investor Books will force you to build it because you can not enter a check made payable to anyone until you've entered them as a vendor.

Speed Button — VENDOR (Pro 2006 Users)

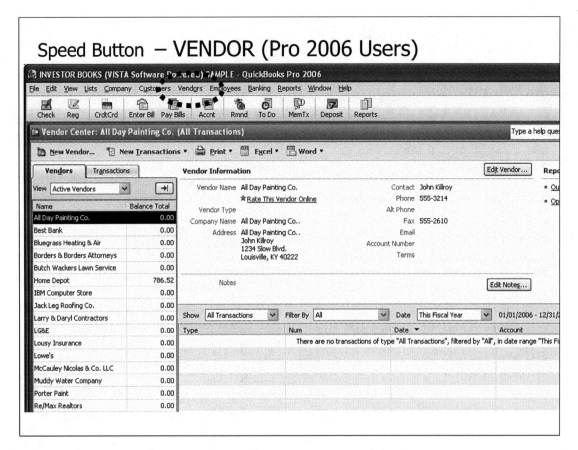

Quickbooks Pro 2006 does not allow the Vendor Speed Button to be displayed on your ICON Bar.

You must click on the VENDORS name in your tool bar and click on Vendors.

Although, this has a different look, you still just tap the keys on your keyboard to who ever you're searching for.

For example, just touch "HOM" and it will immediately jump to Home Depot.

As a rule of thumb, we don't like changes and I agree, but there is a lot of information available to us on this one screen.

This is one of the biggest changes in 2006.

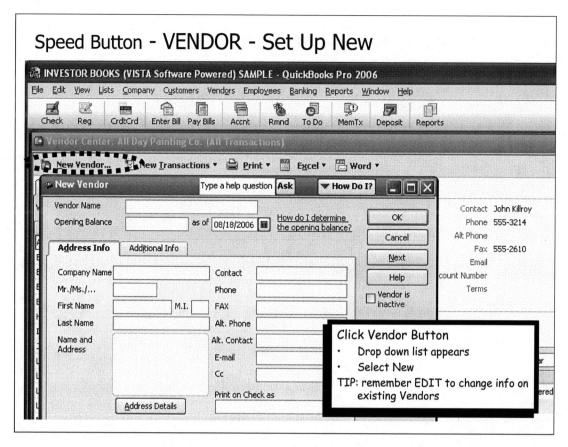

Speed Button - VENDOR - Set Up New

To set up a new vendor and all of their contact information, click on the vendor button found in the lower left corner.

Select new and fill in the blanks.

Again, very user friendly.

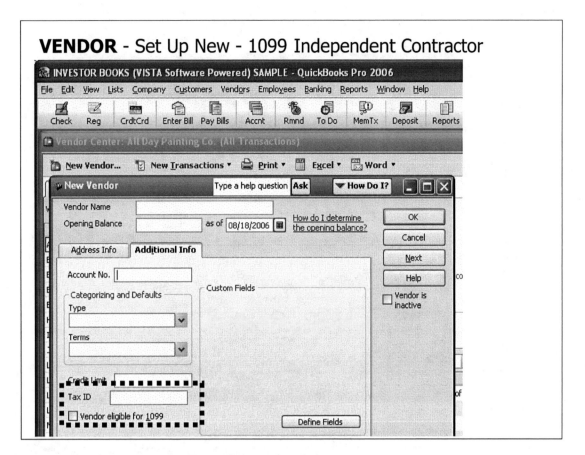

VENDOR - Set Up New - 1099 Independent Contractor

You must enter a Tax ID number

- companies may have their own.

- Individuals – use their Social Security Number.

-Use this at the end of each, just push a button

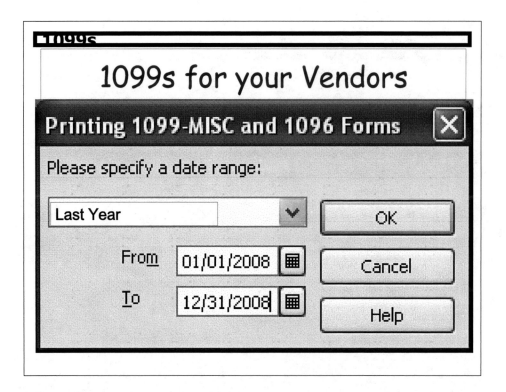

1099s for your Vendors

Printing 1099-MISC and 1096 Forms

Please specify a date range:

Last Year

From 01/01/2008
To 12/31/2008

OK
Cancel
Help

Get your forms from Office Depot or Staples, place them in your printer and hit the print button.

To save paper and ink, you might hit preview.

Speed Button - Account

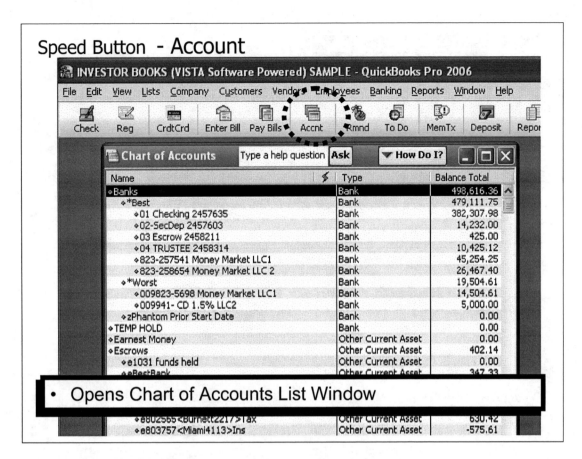

ACCOUNT Speed Button will display your Chart of Accounts

      - the type of account

      - the balance associated with acct.

BANKS are at the top.

Notice the scroll bar on the right.

If you have hundreds of properties this list could be very, very, long.

Speed Button - Reminders

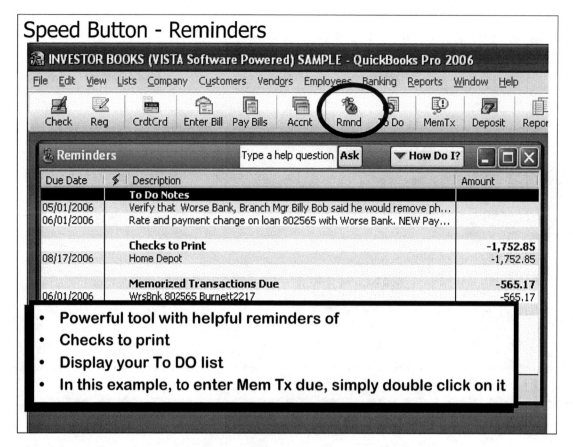

REMINDERS Speed Button displays the

Reminders window and will show you:

- TO DO's scheduled or PAST DUE

- checks to print

- transactions due

- bills to pay

Good tool to help you stay on top of things.

Excellent personal helper and reminder too, birthdays, anniversaries, valentines day, etc.

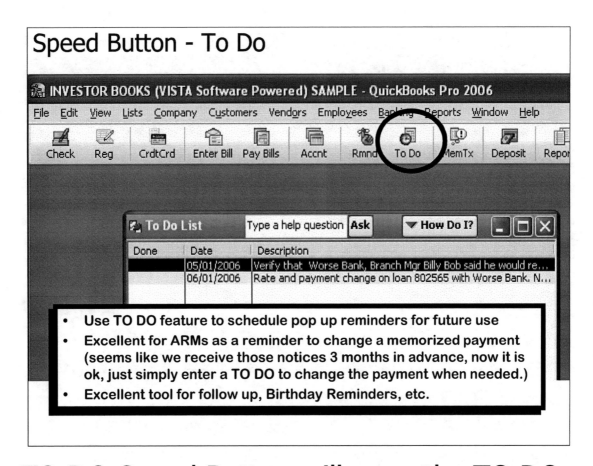

Speed Button - To Do

(Screenshot content: INVESTOR BOOKS (VISTA Software Powered) SAMPLE - QuickBooks Pro 2006)

Toolbar: Check | Reg | CrdtCrd | Enter Bill | Pay Bills | Accnt | Rmnd | To Do | MemTx | Deposit | Repo...

To Do List — Type a help question [Ask] ▼ How Do I?

Done	Date	Description
	05/01/2006	Verify that Worse Bank, Branch Mgr Billy Bob said he would re...
	06/01/2006	Rate and payment change on loan 802565 with Worse Bank. N...

- Use TO DO feature to schedule pop up reminders for future use
- Excellent for ARMs as a reminder to change a memorized payment (seems like we receive those notices 3 months in advance, now it is ok, just simply enter a TO DO to change the payment when needed.)
- Excellent tool for follow up, Birthday Reminders, etc.

TO DO Speed Button will open the TO DO window.

You can create, edit, make inactive, or mark done, TO DO's.

They are sorted in chronological order.

USER TIP: KEEP THIS LIST CURRENT.

Do NOT let it grOW. It will become an albatross and will be useless.

Speed Button - MEMORIZED TRANSACTIONS

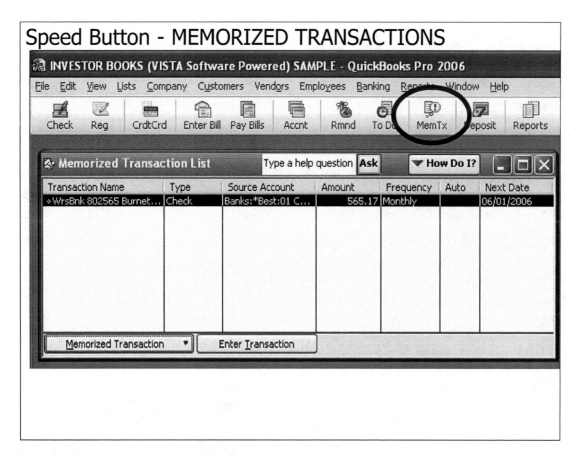

MemTX Speed Button displays your list of memorized transactions.

IMPORTANT: You can NOT create memorized transactions here.

You MUST CREATE the transaction before you can memorize it.

Some users have had a bit of trouble and hair pulling sessions

on this one. Make a note on this one.

Remember, Investor Books is set up to automatically REMIND YOU 10 days in advance, so always enter the real due date.

Speed Button - **DEPOSIT**

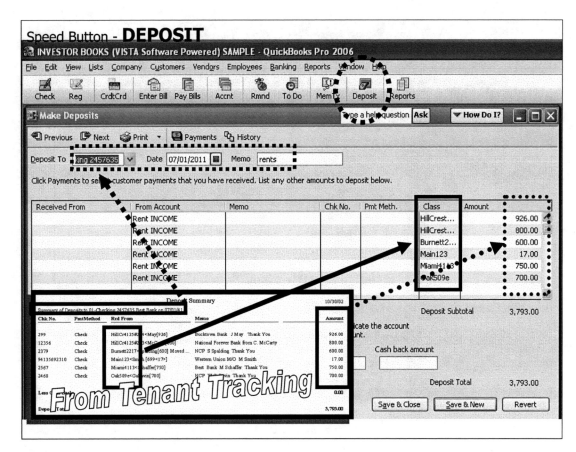

Select Bank Account

   TAB to & Select Date, Memo = rents

   TAB to, Rent Income

   TAB to Class,

   TAB & enter dollar amount

   Select Save & Close

 screens shows in detail how a deposit summary slip created in TENANT TRACKING is used to make an income deposit into Investor Books.

Study a moment, now you can see how it works with Tenant Tracking.

This is great to see this method of sorting data working in BOTH systems for your real estate!

It sets the stage for a good system of checks and balances.

(Reduced opportunity for in house embezzling. Only Deposited Income actually entered into your books.)

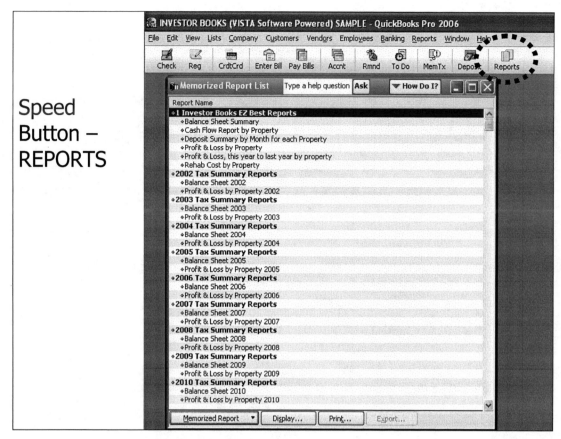

Speed Button – REPORTS

REPORTS Speed Button will open the Memorized Report List window.

Already set up for you are the reports listed above.

If you like a certain report, MEMORIZE IT and place it on this list for future use.

See the Year Tax Summary Reports. You will create your end of year reports, memorize them and place them in the group for the tax year. AWESOME for future reference.

Do not confuse the REPORTS Speed Button with the Reports TOOLBAR.

There are many, many more reports to be found in the toolbar Reports, including the list of memorized reports

Intuit® Terms

Income & Expense Accounts

"CLASS" is the MAGIC !
Use CLASS for each property

We are still on a brief review of Chart of Accounts.

The CLASS feature is the magic making Quickbooks awesome for real estate.

Remember the columns on the profit and loss reports? THOSE WERE CLASSES.

No Need for Rent Income Account for EACH PROPERTY. I have seen it done many times over... STOP IT

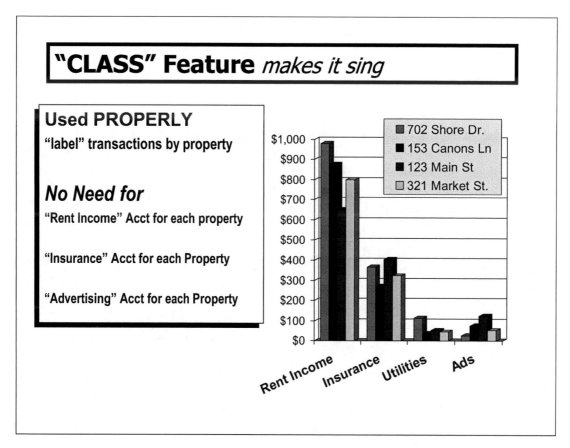

CLASS features allows using one RENT INCOME account for all of your properties.

Allows one Advertising Expense account for all of your properties.

Could be similar to flagging and expense or income with a color flag for each property.

Without the CLASS feature, you would need a Rent Income Account for each property, an Advertising Expense account for each property and so on.

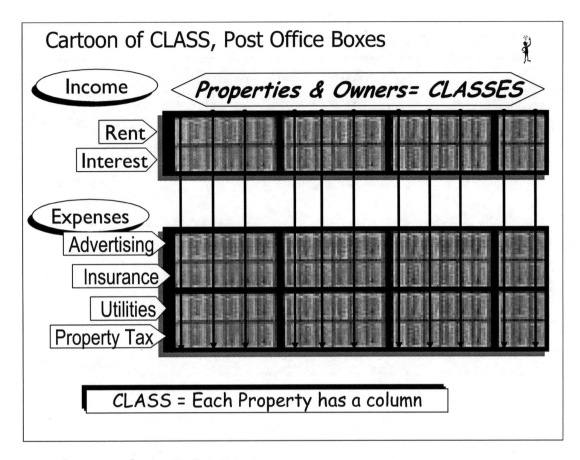

Cartoon of CLASS, Post Office Boxes

Income

Properties & Owners= CLASSES

Rent
Interest

Expenses
Advertising
Insurance
Utilities
Property Tax

CLASS = Each Property has a column

Back to the PO Box...

Classes are the COLUMNS

The name for each column would be a CLASS

(To expand on this idea a bit, if you wanted to group some together, you name the group a CLASS by the group name, and each property would become a SUB CLASS of the CLASS)

Column Names are used for Property Names and Owner Names

Profit and Loss by CLASS Report

	HillcrstApts (LLC1)	Main123 (LLC1)	Miami4113 (LLC1)	Total LLC1	TOTAL
Income					
Rent	77,477.90	6,720.00	6,443.80	90,641.70	90,641.70
Total Income	77,477.90	6,720.00	6,443.80	90,641.70	90,641.70
Gross Profit	77,477.90	6,720.00	6,443.80	90,641.70	90,641.70
Expense					
Capitalized	5,572.34	0.00	0.00	5,572.34	5,572.34
Cleaning & Maintenance	5,210.87	0.00	0.00	5,210.87	5,210.87
Dues & Subscriptions	24.00	0.00	0.00	24.00	24.00
Insurance	4,100.78	525.29	230.60	4,856.67	4,856.67
IntExp					
Mortgage	34,365.11	2,428.32	2,102.76	38,896.19	38,896.19
Total IntExp	34,365.11	2,428.32	2,102.76	38,896.19	38,896.19
L & P	452.00	0.00	0.00	452.00	452.00
Management	-225.00	0.00	0.00	-225.00	-225.00
Repairs	8,731.44	476.18	245.30	9,452.92	9,452.92
Taxes					
Property	4,182.72	444.33	577.38	5,204.43	5,204.43
Total Taxes	4,182.72	444.33	577.38	5,204.43	5,204.43
Utilities	14,330.55	0.00	0.00	14,330.55	14,330.55
Total Expense	76,744.81	3,874.12	3,156.04	83,774.97	83,774.97
Net Income	**733.09**	**2,845.88**	**3,287.76**	**6,866.73**	**6,866.73**

The COLUMN Names are your CLASSES

In the example shown:

    Hillcrest Apts is a SUB CLASS of

    LLC1 (which is a class)

This is a good example of "grouping" specific properties together.

Create Your Chart of Accounts

for your Investor Books.
- This involves setting up your
  - Bank accounts
  - Properties
  - Loans
  - Credit Card Accounts

- Let's Start with Bank Accounts......

Earlier, you quickly reviewed the Chart of Accounts already set up for you in Investor Books.

One major problem here.

You must add your bank accounts, loans, properties, and more.

You will add your stuff to everything EXCEPT the Income and Expense accounts.

(We got those from the IRS.)

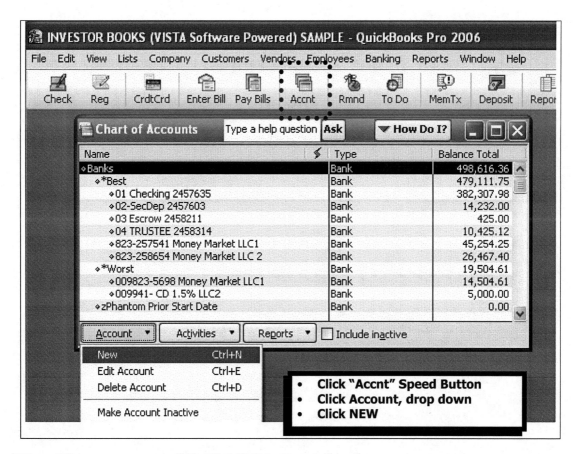

To Enter or CREATE Bank Accounts.

Click on the ACCNT Speed Button

The Chart of Accounts will be displayed.

The Bank accounts are always at the top.

Select the Account Button.

A Drop down list appears.

Select NEW

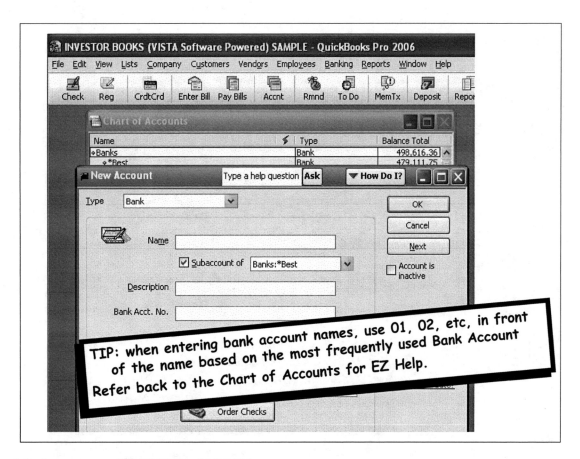

Make sure TYPE is BANK.

TAB thru each field.

IMPORTANT: your first new bank account should be BANKS. Do NOT make your bank accounts sub-accounts of the existing BANKS account already set up. If you do this, QB will combine the existing phantom sample balances with yours and you will not be happy.

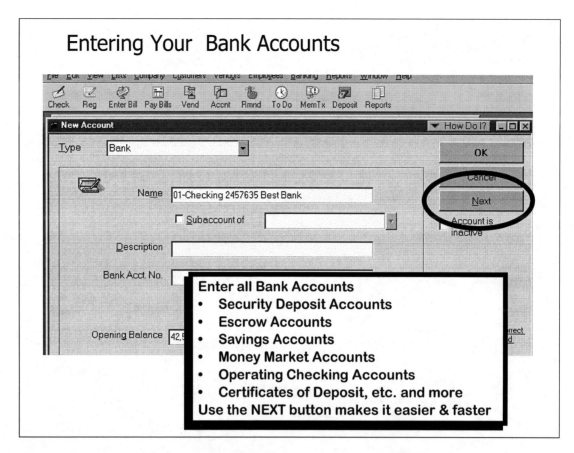

Entering Your Bank Accounts

Enter all Bank Accounts
- **Security Deposit Accounts**
- **Escrow Accounts**
- **Savings Accounts**
- **Money Market Accounts**
- **Operating Checking Accounts**
- **Certificates of Deposit, etc. and more**

Use the NEXT button makes it easier & faster

Use the NEXT button if you are creating a number of new accounts in getting started.

It will makes things go a lot faster for you.

Pick a Target Date FIRST for entire file.

> for example, avoid having half of it set up by a certain date, make it ALL active by a certain date.

As you enter dollar amounts into already in use or already set up Accounts, use "Opening Balance" account as the source of getting that dollar amount of money into the account.

This applies for all accounts that have a balance. (Bank, Asset, Liability, etc.)

> This helps you get "up and running" more quickly.

Entering Your Properties

Enter Your Properties in 2 places.
- Real Estate Properties = Fixed Assets
  - Enter in FIXED Asset Accounts
- Create a CLASS list of properties
  - Used with Income and Expense Accounts
  - Remember the COLUMNS in P&L Reports and Post Office? You will name or title each column

Start with Asset Accounts and enter your properties.

Remember the COLUMNS in the Profit and Loss Report and the Post Office Cartoon? You will name each column here.

Properties you own will be FIXED ASSETS.

Make them sub-accounts of the year purchased.

Properties will also become CLASSES.

If you do not have any LLCs or other entities, enter each property as a class.

Create a CLASS, such as your initials for income and expenses not associated with a specific property. Such things as telephone, cell phone, business cards, education, etc, are all investment expenses not associated with a particular property; however, you can NOT enter a transaction without a CLASS.

Setting up Your Properties as Fixed Assets

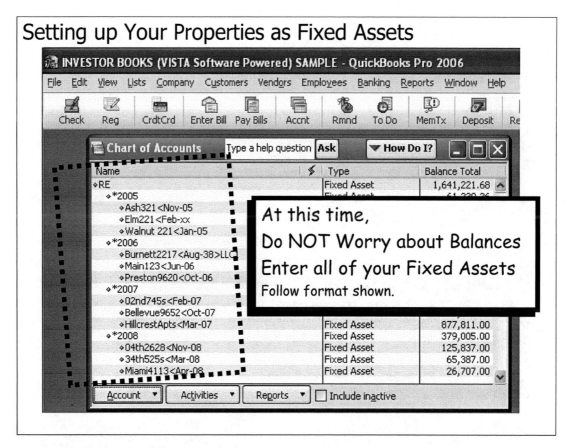

Your Chart of Accounts will start to come together and fixed assets will be sorted by the year purchased.

This may seem like a lot of work, but remember, you are just getting this set up.

You will only enter each Fixed Asset one time and be done.

Do not worry about balances at this time.

Make sure you select proper account type.

<u>Following this format is Fantastic!</u>

Allows You to see

      Total <u>invested</u> in Real Estate

      Sorted by Year of Acquisition

      View Yearly total

      View Yearly acquired properties

As they are sold, balance will be ZERO'd out, but stay put here.

Setting up Your Properties w CLASSES

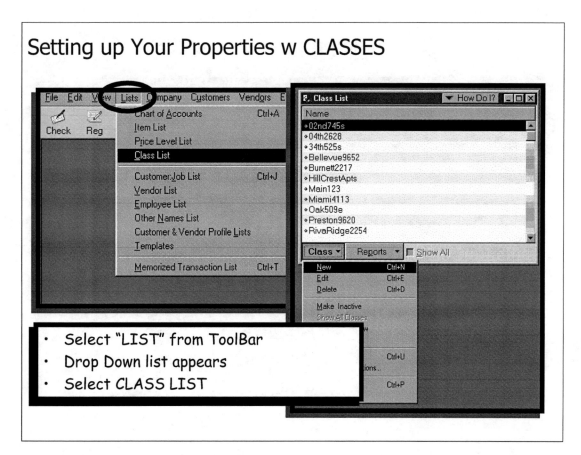

(Naming the columns as seen earlier in P&L Reports)

Do you have single member LLCs and do NOT have to file a separate tax return and the LLC activity exists for liability purposes and does not exist for tax purposes? If yes, create a class for each single member LLC, and make each property a sub class of each LLC.

If you do not have LLCs, simply create a class for each property as displayed in the screen above.

Remember to create a CLASS for YOU, for things not associated to a specific property.

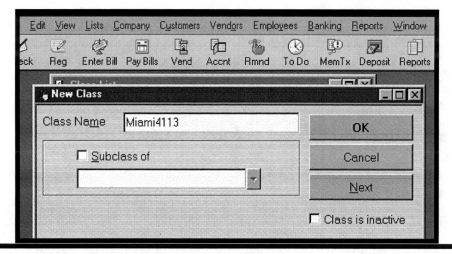

CLASS - Setting up properties - CLASSES

Remember, CLASS feature is powerful.
EVERY TRANSACTION <u>MUST</u> HAVE A CLASS

Class is what make this work for Real Estate Investors.

Every transaction you enter MUST have a class.

UNCLASSIFIED transactions will turn your system into garbage.

Again, this is the COLUMN Name as viewed earlier in Profit and Loss Reports.

SINGLE MEMBER LLCs

Each entity filing a TAX Return must have it's own books.

SINGLE MEMBER LLC

Single Member LLC's are catching on for real estate investors.

Set up properly, You may elect to have them not exist for IRS Tax purposes

You may choose to have them exist for liability concerns only.

If set up and used this way, this allows the opportunity for several LLCs to exist in one company file (1 Tax Return)

Set up properly, several LLCs can exist in your Investor Books company file (1 Tax Return)

This can be achieved easily in QB with just a few modifications to the format - sorting data ground rules.

modifications to format - sorting data ground rules.

INCOME & EXPENSE Accounts

Add **"Paid to Owners"** Expense Account

Asset Accounts

Add Bank Accounts for each LLC

Add LLC initials to name of each Asset for the LLC

Liability Accounts - Add LLC initials somewhere in the name

CLASSes

Make each Owner a CLASS **(Use your Initials if you have no entities)**

Makes each Property a "Sub-Class" of each owner.

If you do not have any entities such as LLCs or corps,

- create a Class using your Initials. (mine would be *mb)

- **For example, if I did not have any entities, I would create a class named MB for Mike Butler and use the Class MB for purchases and income not property specific. Such things as gas for car, business cards, cell phones, office supplies, etc.**

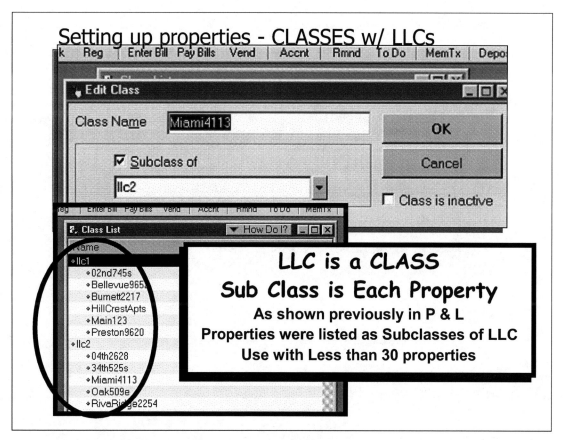

Setting up properties - CLASSES w/ LLCs

LLC is a CLASS
Sub Class is Each Property
As shown previously in P & L
Properties were listed as Subclasses of LLC
Use with Less than 30 properties

This allows for a Profit & Loss Report sorted by

each LLC

each property owned by an LLC

Total for each LLC

Total for ALL PROPERTIES

Use this if you expect to have less than 20 Properties (not units).

If you have more than 20 properties

Or you expect to have more than 20
USE THE FOLLOWING SYSTEM.

Class Name

<StreetName><HouseNumber><Initial of LLC>

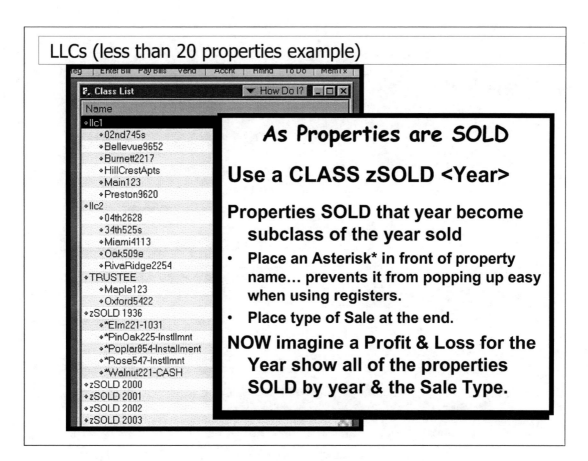

LLCs (less than 20 properties example)

As Properties are SOLD

Use a CLASS zSOLD <Year>

Properties SOLD that year become subclass of the year sold

- Place an Asterisk* in front of property name… prevents it from popping up easy when using registers.
- Place type of Sale at the end.

NOW imagine a Profit & Loss for the Year show all of the properties SOLD by year & the Sale Type.

For your review, you will see classes already set up for sold properties.

As you sell properties, they will become subclasses of year sold.

The "z" in front forces them to be displayed at the bottom of the Class List and they will be displayed last on your Profit and Loss Report for the year.

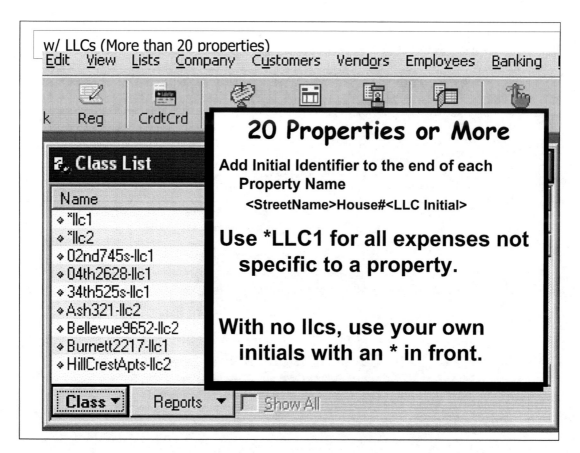

20 or more properties. Use the format above.

Notice the *"*llc1"* used for income and expenses not specific to a property, such as phone bills, yard signs, office supplies, etc.

IF you do not have an LLC,

simply use your OWN initials.

For example, without any llcs, and using my name, I would have a class named *"*mb"* for tracking income and expenses related to real estate, but not property specific.

EARNEST MONEY (Good Faith Deposit)

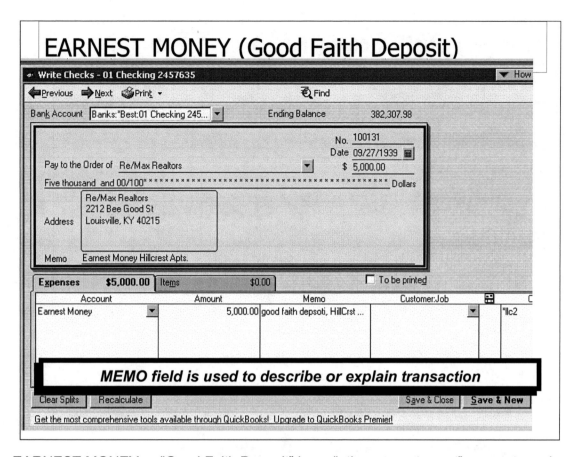

EARNEST MONEY or "Good Faith Deposit" is an "other current asset" account used to hold your money pending successful purchase closing of a property.

CLASS used will be the entity making the offer. If you have no entity, use the class named with your initials.

Earnest Money is usually with an offer to purchase.

In the real world, it is generally not accepted or deposited unless the offer is accepted.

Your Earnest Money is usually deposited into a broker's escrow account.

INVESTMENT TIP:

You could give a FSBO Seller an earnest money check; however, keep in mind, that if they pull a George Jones NO SHOW at closing, you could be left holding the bag.

It is recommended to never make earnest money check payable directly to the FSBO Seller, make it payable to your closing attorney AND the FSBO Seller…

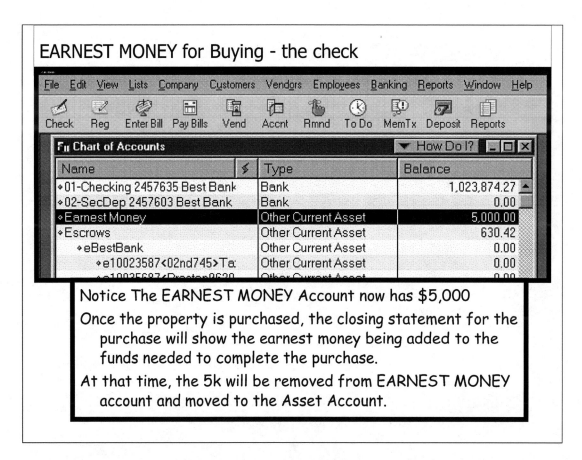

EARNEST MONEY for Buying - the check

Notice The EARNEST MONEY Account now has $5,000

Once the property is purchased, the closing statement for the purchase will show the earnest money being added to the funds needed to complete the purchase.

At that time, the 5k will be removed from EARNEST MONEY account and moved to the Asset Account.

Earnest Money is NOT an EXPENSE.

You have not purchased anything.. *YET.*

You are trying to buy a property and someone is holding YOUR MONEY until this occurs.

Therefore, you have NOT spent it, it is being held by someone else.

Kind of sounds like an escrow account where a lender is holding YOUR MONEY to pay taxes or insurance later.... Very similar, it is still YOUR MONEY they are holding.

Closing Statements

Generally is a summary of the details involved in
- buying, selling, exchanging real estate
- Borrowing money or lending money on real estate
- Before starting, make sure
  - all accounts involved are set up properly
- Does NOT have to be the formal HUD 1 form.
- It could be homemade, scribbled on a napkin, or on a post it note.

This is by far the most difficult procedure for investors to handle in way that your CPA or accountant will approve.

Building on all of the previous things, I hope to make CLOSING STATEMENTS a very simple process.

You will break it down into baby steps.

A Closing Statement is nothing more than a giant split transaction.. Remember the Post Office if it helps you and you will be fine.

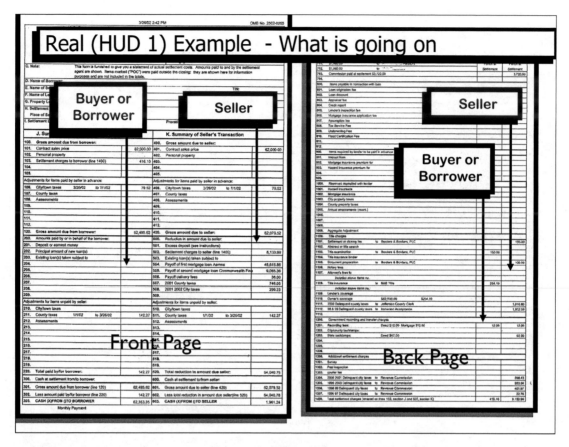

Learn the parts first. Most closings use a HUD 1, a government form used to document the detail of a real estate transaction or loan.

It has a front page and a back page.

It has a BUYER / Borrower Column

It has a Seller Column if a Seller is involved.

As you can see, there are many lines on this form. IT seems there are many title companies, lenders, and attorneys who try to make sure all the lines get filled.

Try to get these in advance of your closing and preview them, challenge ANYTHING you do not understand or agree with on the statement.

> **Regardless of the activity...**
>
> # If You BRING Money
> ## Start with a Check
>
> # If You Get Money
> ## Start with a DEPOSIT

BEFORE you start.

MEMORIZE

these phrases

It will keep you on track and out of trouble.

They will save you money and grief.

Perhaps write it down on a post it note and stick it to your computer.

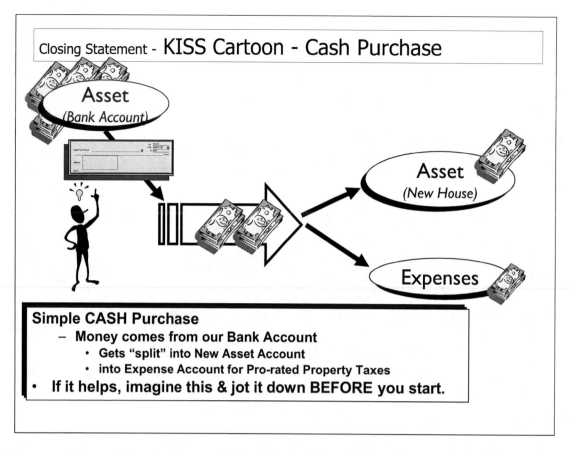

Closing Statement - KISS Cartoon - Cash Purchase

Asset
(Bank Account)

Asset
(New House)

Expenses

Simple CASH Purchase
- **Money comes from our Bank Account**
  - **Gets "split" into New Asset Account**
  - **into Expense Account for Pro-rated Property Taxes**
- **If it helps, imagine this & jot it down BEFORE you start.**

The cartoon listed above is intended to help illustrate what is going on with the closing statement.

Remember the Post Office accounts.

A simple CASH purchase of real estate should cause you to write a check at closing resulting in the purchase of a NEW asset along with some money going to the Expense account of Property Taxes (usually pro-rated to the closing date between Buyer and Seller)

If the closing statement and computer screens seem a bit overwhelming, simply draw yourself a cartoon of what is going on. Ask yourself, "what is going on here?, what account will be involved?"

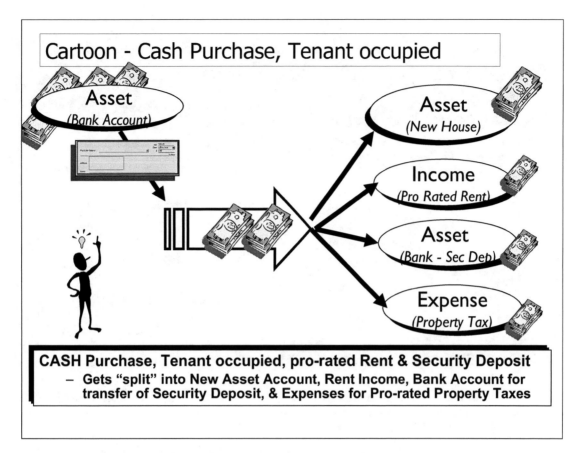

This cartoon is an example of:

Cash Purchase

Tenant Occupied, (pro-rated rent)

Tenant has Security Deposit

Expense of pro-rated Property taxes

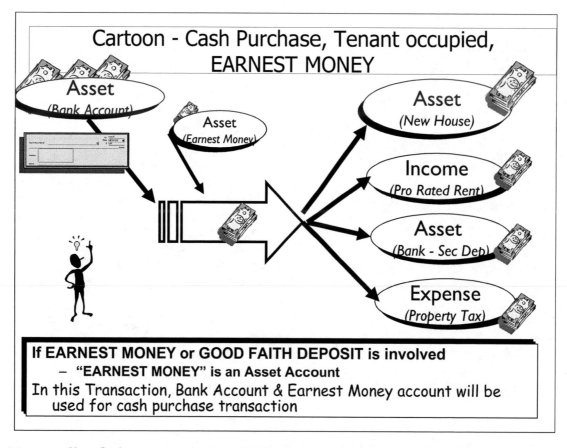

Cartoon - Cash Purchase, Tenant occupied, EARNEST MONEY

Asset
(Bank Account)

Asset
(Earnest Money)

Asset
(New House)

Income
(Pro Rated Rent)

Asset
(Bank - Sec Dep)

Expense
(Property Tax)

If EARNEST MONEY or GOOD FAITH DEPOSIT is involved
– **"EARNEST MONEY" is an Asset Account**
In this Transaction, Bank Account & Earnest Money account will be used for cash purchase transaction

Now all of the previous AND ADD the use of a EARNEST MONEY check for the good faith deposit.

Because you need to take money to the closing, you will start with creating a check and add money from the earnest money account spending it on all of the accounts listed down the right side of the screen.

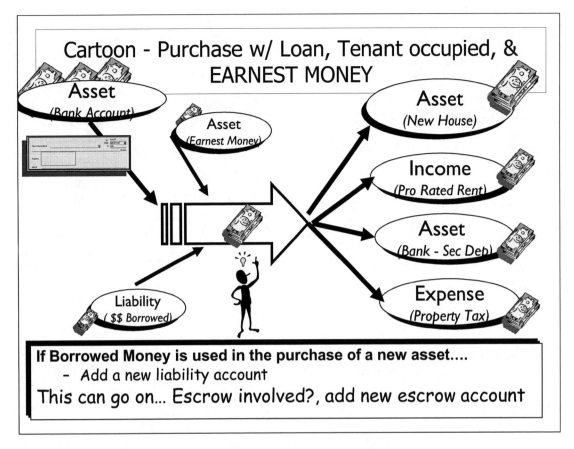

Cartoon - Purchase w/ Loan, Tenant occupied, & EARNEST MONEY

If Borrowed Money is used in the purchase of a new asset....
- Add a new liability account

This can go on... Escrow involved?, add new escrow account

Let's everything described before and USE A BRAND NEW LOAN to help with the purchase...

Again, because you are taking money to closing, you start with a check and combine it with EARNEST MONEY and the new LIABILITY account (new loan) and spend it on the accounts listed down the right side of the screen.

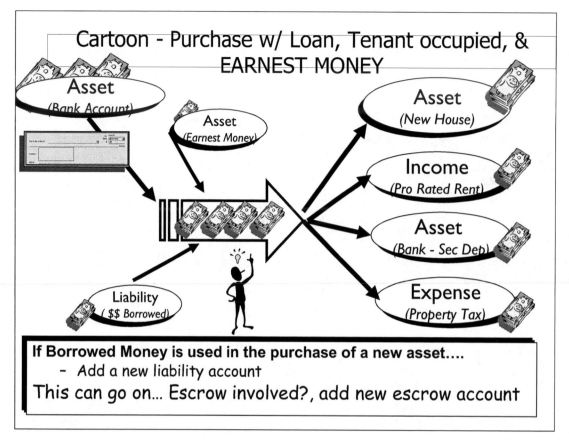

This can go on and on...

You could have an escrow account involved with the new loan.... See what I mean..

The point is to STOP and ask yourself "What is going on here, and what accounts are needed to enter the closing statement properly."

If you will discipline yourself to do this with each closing statement, just like a pilot goes through a checklist before take off, IT WILL BECOME EASY, even the most complicated closing statement you could imagine, can be broken down into baby steps.

CASH PURCHASE of a House

- Make sure accounts are set up
  - Bank Account
  - Create Fixed Asset Account for House
  - Create "CLASS" for this House

- *Let's assume the bank account already exists*
  - *Next step is to enter the House as a New Fixed Asset*
  - *Address of the property is **2217 Burnett***

Make sure all of the accounts involved are set up.

You must create a new

> Fixed Asset
>
> Class

BUYING - CASH Purchase

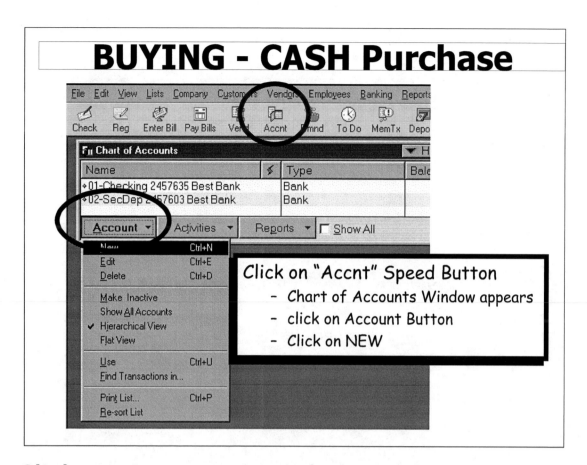

Click on "Accnt" Speed Button
- Chart of Accounts Window appears
- click on Account Button
- Click on NEW

Click on Account Speed Button.

Click on Account Button

Select New

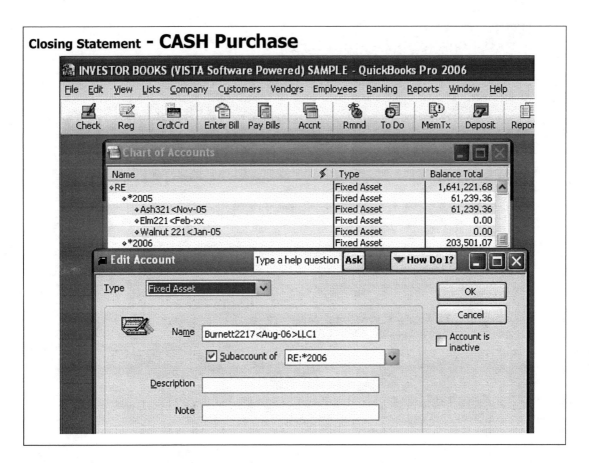

Closing Statement - CASH Purchase

Fill in the fields properly

Make the new Fixed Asset a sub-account of the year purchased.

Enter the name of your new Fixed Asset

Remember to follow the format

<StreetName><HouseNumber><Month-Year>

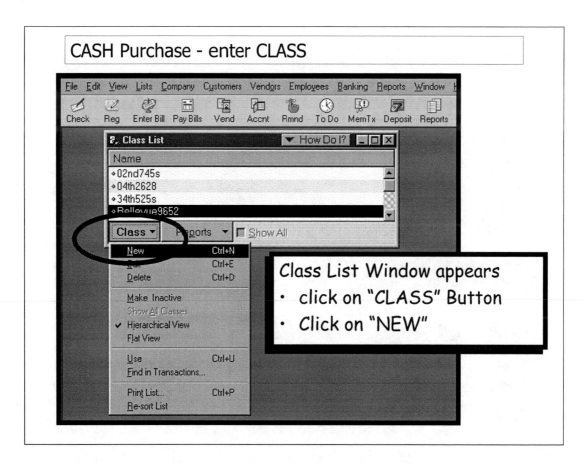

At the top, in the TOOLBAR, click on LISTS and select CLASS.

The Class List window will be displayed.

Click on the Class button, select NEW and enter your new class following the same name FORMAT.

\<StreetName\>\<HouseNumber\>

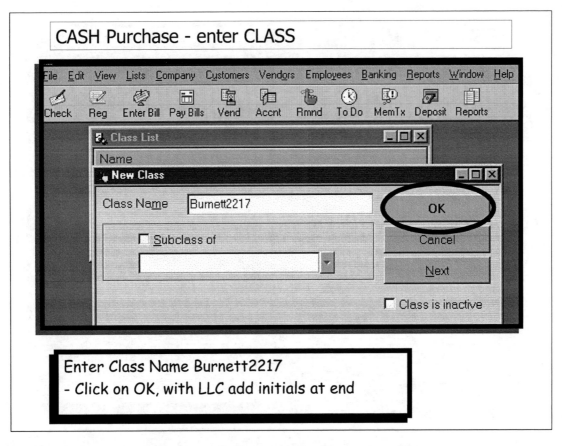

CASH Purchase - enter CLASS

Enter Class Name Burnett2217
- Click on OK, with LLC add initials at end

Click on OK, You successfully entered a new class.

When you hear CLASS, think Property.

Verify that you are ready to enter the transaction of cash purchase of 2217 Burnett

Fixed Asset Account **Burnett2217 < Aug-06**

CLASS is set up   **Burnett2217**

NOW Ready to enter the purchase

2 Things are Needed

    CLOSING STATEMENT

    Write a check for the purchase

    Let's Review the CLOSING STATEMENT 1st

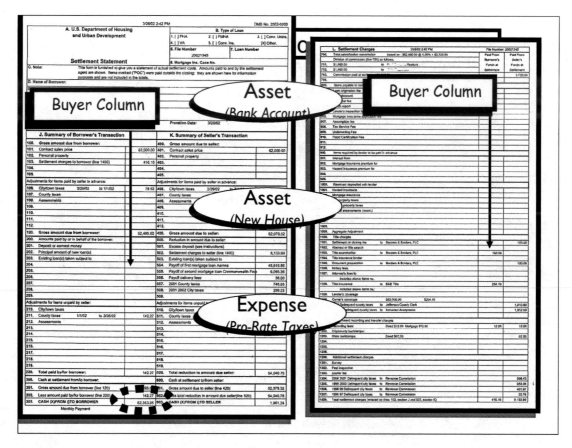

Think again about what is going on here.

Identify YOUR COLUMN.

If it helps, write or circle it, use a highlighter…. Whatever helps you, use it.

Look at the bottom of the front page.

This number located here will tell you how much money to take to closing (or receive).

This is the amount you will write a check for to begin this transaction.

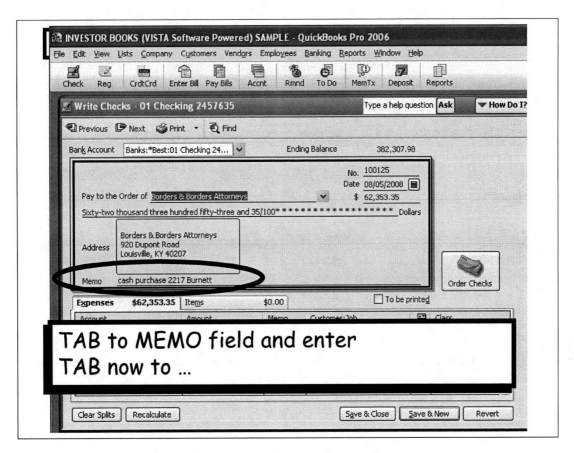

Click on the CHECK Speed Button and select the proper bank account.

TAB to enter the proper date.

TAB to payee (vendor) and do the same.

TAB to dollar amount field and enter the amount noted on bottom of PAGE 1 from closing statement.

TAB to MEMO field and enter what this check involves. Describe in 3-5 words to your CPA. Something like Cash Purchase of 2217 Burnett will work.

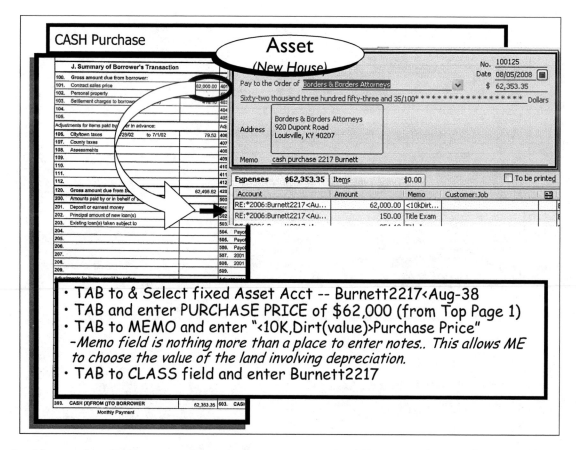

Let's make it easy on your tax prepaper. Remember, they will be reviewing this for your taxes. Helping them out will save you money.

Make this top line the PURCHASE PRICE.

In the account field, select the new fixed asset account you just created.

TAB to enter the PURCHASE PRICE

TAB to MEMO field and enter the dirt value inside the brackets **<10Kdirt>Purchase Price**

TAB to Class and enter the proper class

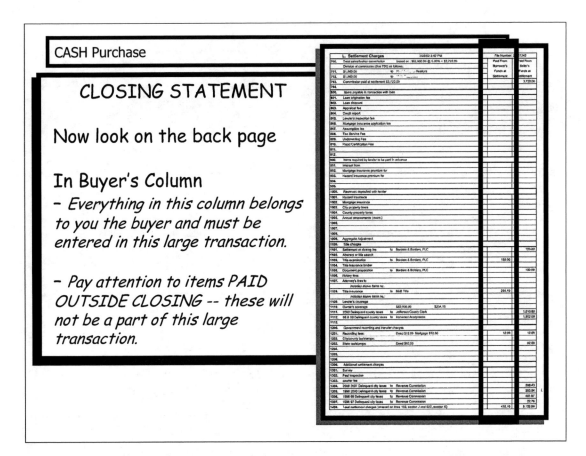

After entering the purchase price on the top line, flip over to the back page of the closing statement.

Identify your column and review the amounts listed.

PAY CLOSE ATTENTION and do NOT include dollar amounts involved in things OUTSIDE OF THIS CLOSING. Many title companies and attorneys put dollar amounts of items prepaid in advance or others.

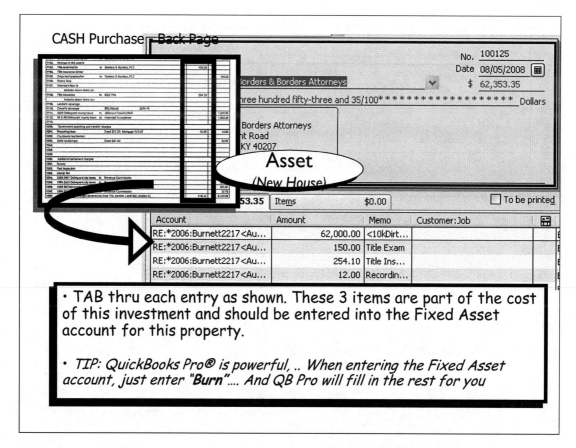

CASH Purchase - Back Page

Asset
(New House)

Account	Amount	Memo	Customer:Job	
RE:*2006:Burnett2217<Au...	62,000.00	<10kDirt...		
RE:*2006:Burnett2217<Au...	150.00	Title Exam		
RE:*2006:Burnett2217<Au...	254.10	Title Ins...		
RE:*2006:Burnett2217<Au...	12.00	Recordin...		

• TAB thru each entry as shown. These 3 items are part of the cost of this investment and should be entered into the Fixed Asset account for this property.

• TIP: QuickBooks Pro® is powerful, .. When entering the Fixed Asset account, just enter "**Burn**".... And QB Pro will fill in the rest for you

Since this is a CASH PURCHASE of real estate, these charges found on the back page are all part of the acquisition cost of our new asset.

Therefore, these dollar amounts will go into the new fixed asset account also.

Remember to use CLASS on each line.

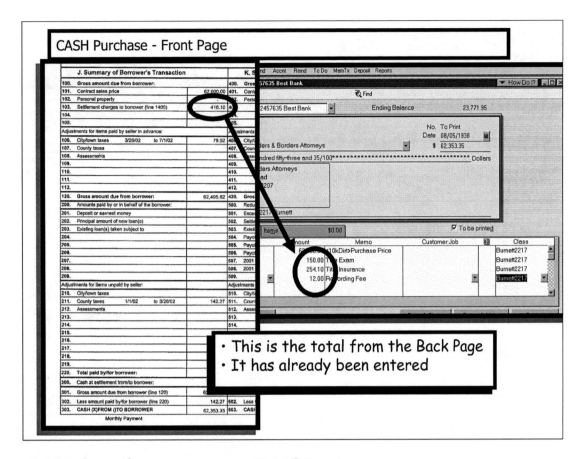

CASH Purchase - Front Page

- This is the total from the Back Page
- It has already been entered

FLIP back over to PAGE 1.

Here you will see the total of page 2 listed on the front page. No need to enter this, you just did.

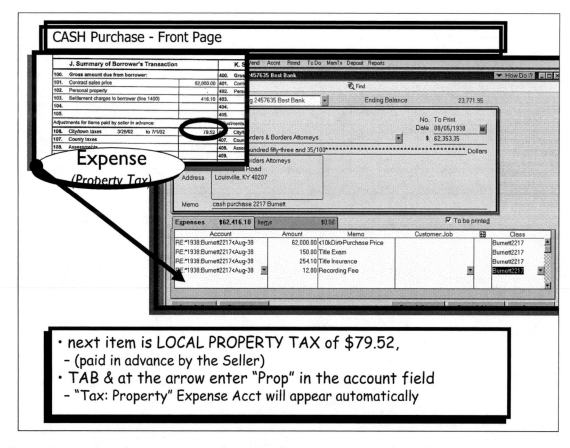

CASH Purchase - Front Page

- next item is LOCAL PROPERTY TAX of $79.52,
  – (paid in advance by the Seller)
- TAB & at the arrow enter "Prop" in the account field
  – "Tax: Property" Expense Acct will appear automatically

Next up in this example, is the pro-ration of property taxes.

PROPERTY TAXES are an EXPENSE and are not part of your acquisition cost.

Do NOT try to argue about it. It won't work.

Question: I buy properties with delinquent property taxes, isn't this part of my acquisition cost?"

ANSWER: You are reading the wrong column on the closing statement. Delinquent property taxes should be listed in the SELLER's column as funds removed from the sale price.

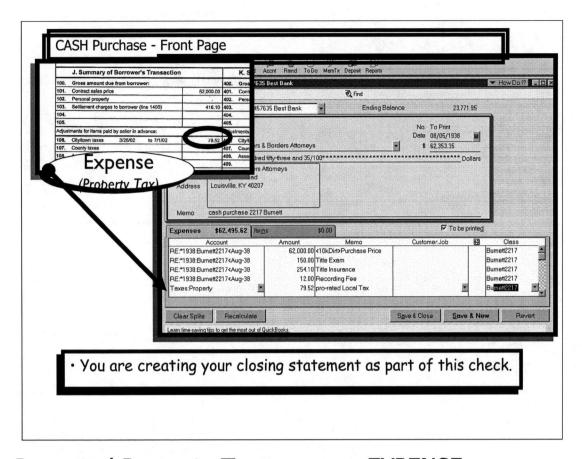

- You are creating your closing statement as part of this check.

Pro-rated Property Taxes are an EXPENSE.

Enter it properly.

Sometimes there are local, state taxes, etc.

You may receive money here, or they may charge you, just read the little bit of text above the section.

If it reads, Items PAID IN ADVANCE BY SELLER, you will be charged for these.

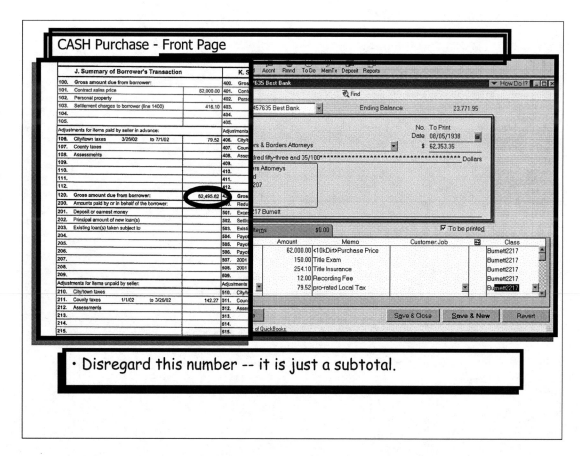

CASH Purchase - Front Page

J. Summary of Borrower's Transaction		
100.	Gross amount due from borrower:	
101.	Contract sales price	62,000.00
102.	Personal property	.
103.	Settlement charges to borrower (line 1400)	416.10
104.		
105.		
Adjustments for items paid by seller in advance:		
106.	City/town taxes 3/26/02 to 7/1/02	79.52
107.	County taxes	
108.	Assessments	
109.		
110.		
111.		
112.		
120.	Gross amount due from borrower:	62,495.62
200.	Amounts paid by or in behalf of the borrower:	
201.	Deposit or earnest money	
202.	Principal amount of new loan(s)	
203.	Existing loan(s) taken subject to	
204.		
205.		
206.		
207.		
208.		
209.		
Adjustments for items unpaid by seller:		
210.	City/town taxes	
211.	County taxes 1/1/02 to 3/26/02	142.27
212.	Assessments	
213.		
214.		
215.		

- Disregard this number -- it is just a subtotal.

Go right down the list of numbers in YOUR COLUMN.

Pay attention, do not confuse SUB TOTALs with dollar amounts to enter in your transaction.

The example above shows a sub total circled. Do not enter it again.

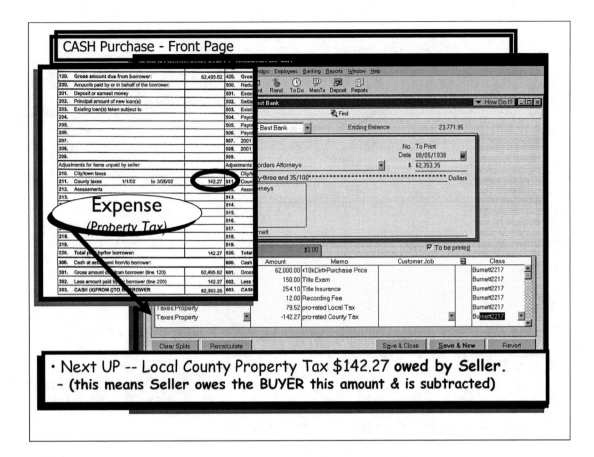

CASH Purchase - Front Page

120.	Gross amount due from borrower:			62,495.62
200.	Amounts paid by or in behalf of the borrower:			
201.	Deposit or earnest money			
202.	Principal amount of new loan(s)			
203.	Existing loan(s) taken subject to			
204.				
205.				
206.				
207.				
208.				
209.				
	Adjustments for items unpaid by seller:			
210.	City/town taxes			
211.	County taxes	1/1/02	to 3/26/02	142.27
212.	Assessments			
213.				
218.				
219.				
220.	Total paid by/for borrower:			142.27
300.	Cash at settlement from/to borrower:			
301.	Gross amount due from borrower (line 120)			62,495.62
302.	Less amount paid by the borrower (line 220)			142.27
303.	CASH (X)FROM ()TO BORROWER			62,353.35

Expense
(Property Tax)

Best Bank — Ending Balance 23,771.95

No. To Print
Date 08/05/1938
$ 62,353.35

...y-three and 35/100************************************ Dollars

☑ To be printed

Amount	Memo	Customer:Job	Class
62,000.00	<10kDirt>Purchase Price		Burnett2217
150.00	Title Exam		Burnett2217
254.10	Title Insurance		Burnett2217
12.00	Recording Fee		Burnett2217
79.52	pro-rated Local Tax		Burnett2217
-142.27	pro-rated County Tax		Burnett2217

Taxes:Property
Taxes:Property

Clear Splits | Recalculate | Save & Close | Save & New | Revert

• Next UP -- Local County Property Tax $142.27 **owed by Seller.**
- (this means Seller owes the BUYER this amount & is subtracted)

This is a real cash purchase closing statement showing both sides of receiving money for property taxes and being charged money for property taxes.

www.MikeButler.com

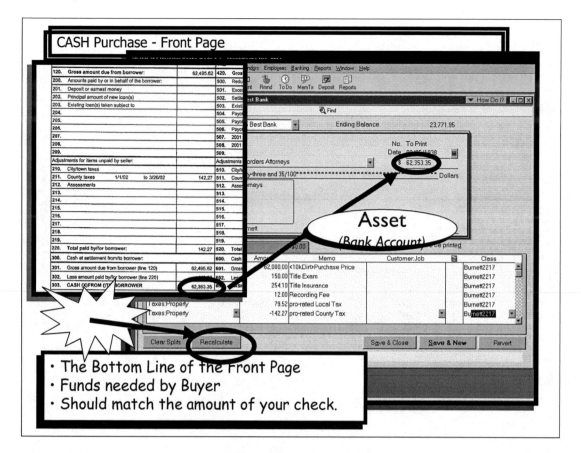

CASH Purchase - Front Page

- The Bottom Line of the Front Page
- Funds needed by Buyer
- Should match the amount of your check.

Use this button. RECALCULATE.

In the beginning you will make mistakes.

Odds are, the first few times, you will unintentionally add extra lines to your transaction and they will scoot down the list. Notice the scroll bar on the far right.

The **recalculate button** helps you to find errors entered. If there are dollar amounts hiding down below, it helps identify those by changing the amount in the dollar field on your check.

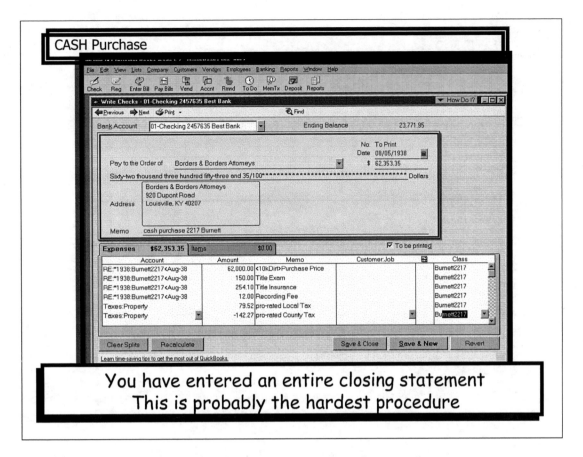

CASH Purchase

You have entered an entire closing statement
This is probably the hardest procedure

Believe it or not, this was the most complicated part.

If you can handle this cash purchase and understand the parts (accounts involved) You will be able to take the most complicated closing statement and break it down to baby steps.

Use whatever it takes to help you understand it. Use the Post Office, draw cartoons, use a highlighter.

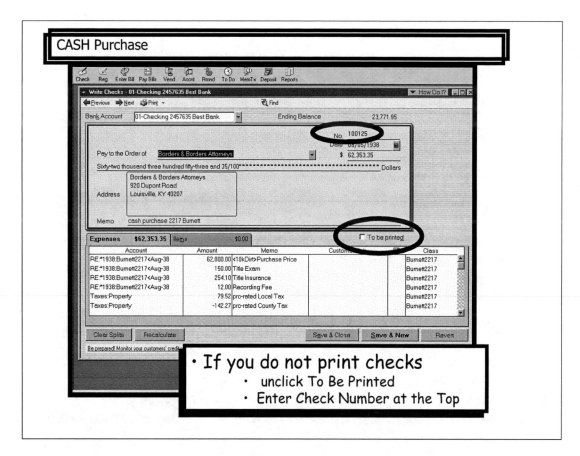

CASH Purchase

- If you do not print checks
  - unclick To Be Printed
  - Enter Check Number at the Top

When your buying machine is cranking and you are moving fast, you usually write a check at the closing.

Either way, if you handwrite your check, be sure and enter the check number in the proper field.

If you are lucky and your closing attorney faxes you the closing statement for your review prior to the closing, you can prepare your check and print it before the closing.

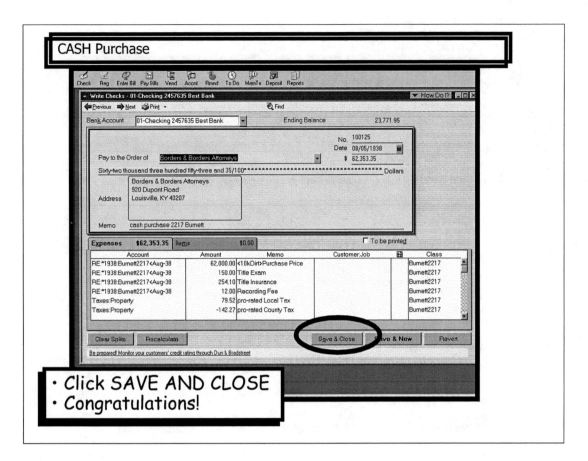

CASH Purchase

- Click SAVE AND CLOSE
- Congratulations!

Be sure and click Save and Close or Save and New.

Do NOT hit the X first. Your entire transaction will get blipped out.

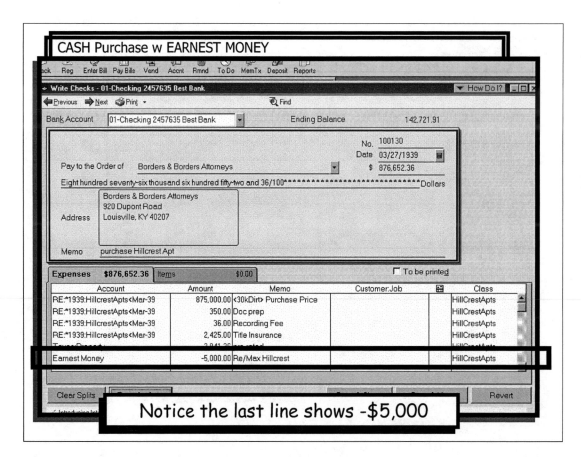

CASH Purchase w EARNEST MONEY

Notice the last line shows -$5,000

You just completed a simple cash purchase in the previous example.

This example will add the use of EARNEST MONEY or good faith deposit.

Remember the cartoon if it helps.

You will pull money from the EARNEST MONEY account to be combined with your other money to pull off the purchase.

The EARNEST Money must be on your closing statement.

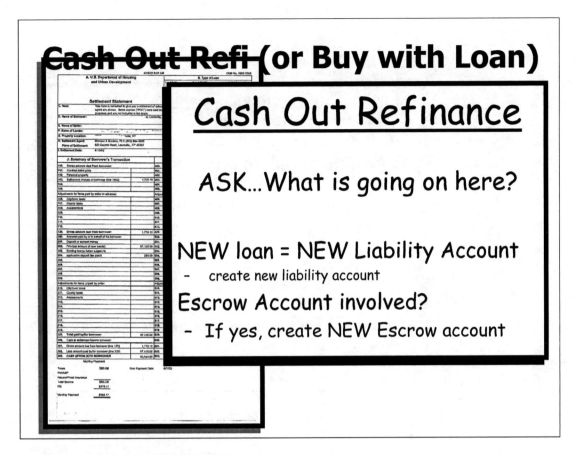

Cash Out Refinance

ASK...What is going on here?

NEW loan = NEW Liability Account
- create new liability account

Escrow Account involved?
- If yes, create NEW Escrow account

CASH OUT REFINANCE

This means NEW MORTGAGE LOAN

You MUST create the new liability account first BEFORE you can use it in a transaction.

If there is an Escrow account involved, you must create if first before you can use it.

You will be DEPOSITING money into a bank account.

This first example assumes you have no existing mortgages or loans on this property. If it did, you would simply have another line to enter noting the dollar amount they used to pay off your existing loan(s).

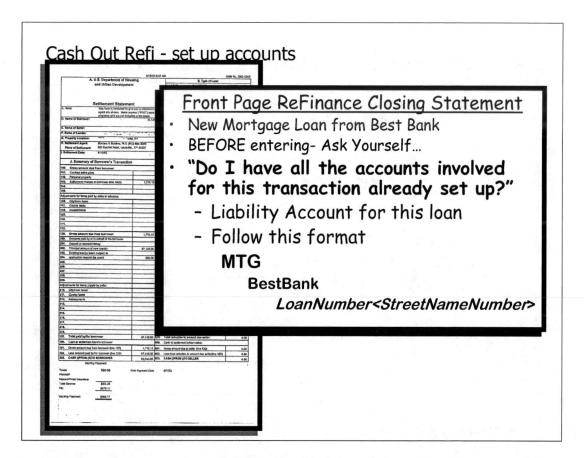

Cash Out Refi - set up accounts

Front Page ReFinance Closing Statement
- New Mortgage Loan from Best Bank
- BEFORE entering- Ask Yourself…
- **"Do I have all the accounts involved for this transaction already set up?"**
  - Liability Account for this loan
  - Follow this format

  MTG

    BestBank

        LoanNumber<StreetNameNumber>

Remember to make liability accounts sub-accounts of the lender involved.

Repeat again, if needed for Escrow accounts.

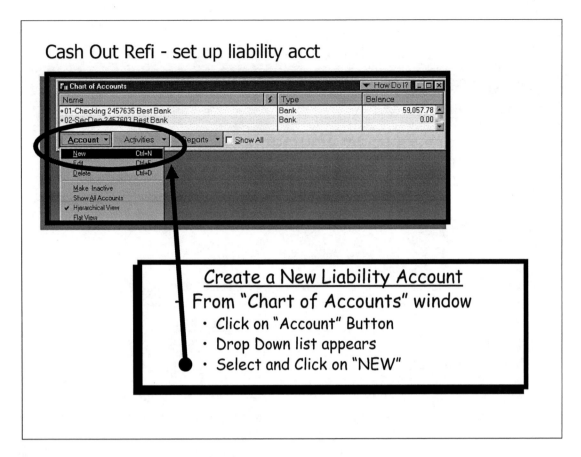

Cash Out Refi - set up liability acct

Create a New Liability Account
- From "Chart of Accounts" window
  - Click on "Account" Button
  - Drop Down list appears
  - Select and Click on "NEW"

To create a Liability Account.

Click on Account Speed Button

Click on Account Button as displayed above.

Select NEW

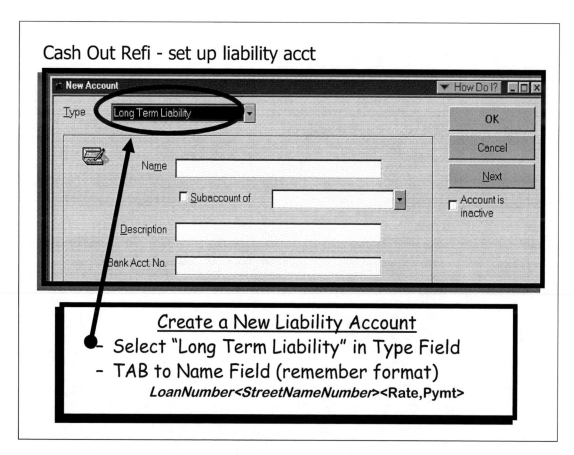

Cash Out Refi - set up liability acct

Create a New Liability Account
- Select "Long Term Liability" in Type Field
- TAB to Name Field (remember format)
  LoanNumber<StreetNameNumber><Rate,Pymt>

In the TYPE field, select LONG TERM LIABILITY.

It will default to BANK, you must change it.

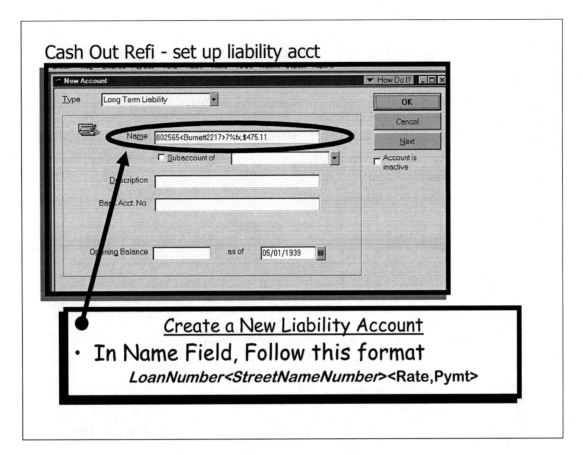

Cash Out Refi - set up liability acct

Create a New Liability Account
- In Name Field, Follow this format
  LoanNumber<StreetNameNumber><Rate,Pymt>

Using the proper format learned earlier, enter the name of the new liability account.

Loan Number<StreetName>Rate,Payment

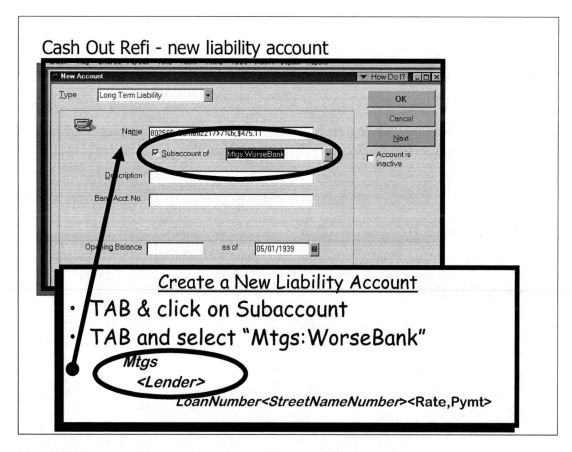

Cash Out Refi - new liability account

Create a New Liability Account
- TAB & click on Subaccount
- TAB and select "Mtgs:WorseBank"

Mtgs
<Lender>
LoanNumber<StreetNameNumber><Rate,Pymt>

TAB to and select sub-account

TAB to and select proper lender.

If the lender is new also, you must create a new liability account just for the lender and then repeat creating the new liability account for the new loan.

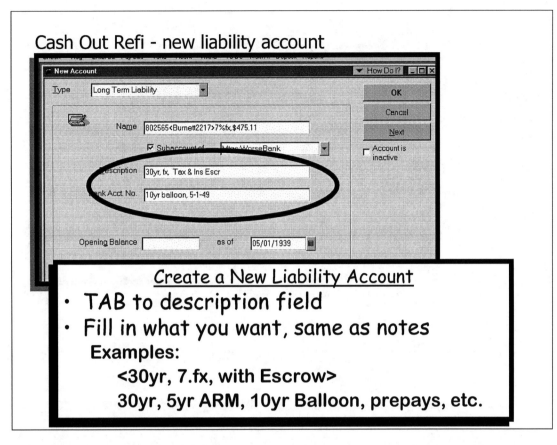

Cash Out Refi - new liability account

Create a New Liability Account
- TAB to description field
- Fill in what you want, same as notes
  Examples:
      <30yr, 7.fx, with Escrow>
      30yr, 5yr ARM, 10yr Balloon, prepays, etc.

The fields labeled description and bank account number – just think of those as little notepads for your self.

You already entered the bank account number in the name of the account, no need to repeat twice.

Enter information that is important to you as an investor.

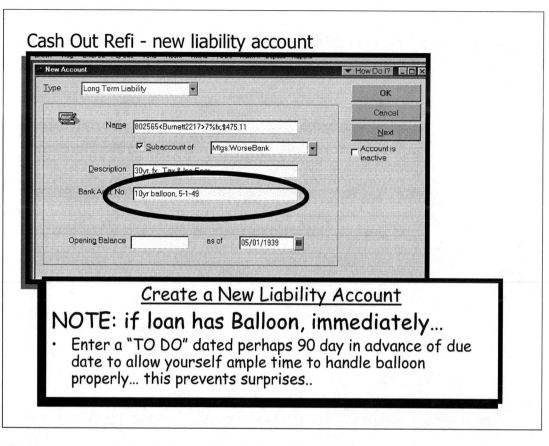

Cash Out Refi - new liability account

Create a New Liability Account
NOTE: if loan has Balloon, immediately...
- Enter a "TO DO" dated perhaps 90 day in advance of due date to allow yourself ample time to handle balloon properly... this prevents surprises..

If your new loan has a balloon, or is an adjustable rate loan, you should immediately go to the TO DO feature of Quickbooks and enter a new TO DO well far in advance of the balloon date to allow you plenty of time to handle it properly.

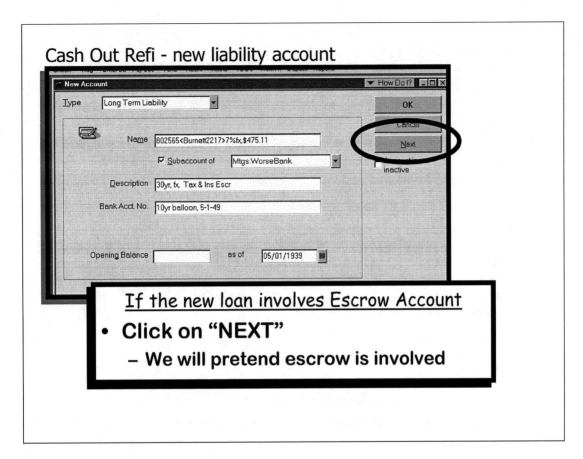

Cash Out Refi - new liability account

If your liability account has an ESCROW account, click on the next button.

Cash Out Refinance w/Escrow

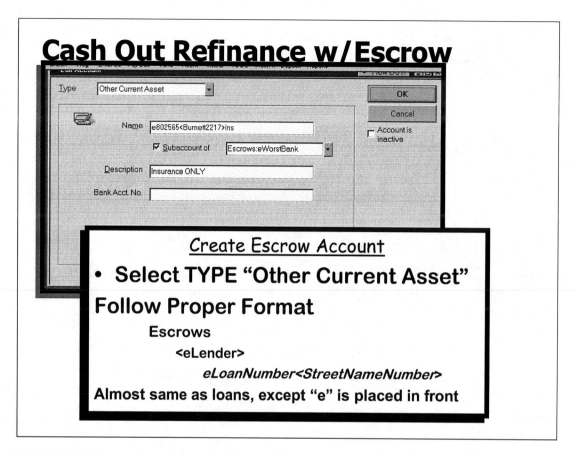

ESCROW accounts

are OTHER CURRENT ASSET

Follow the proper format as noted above.

Everything is almost the same as the liability accounts, except you will place a small "e" in front of the lender name and each escrow account number.

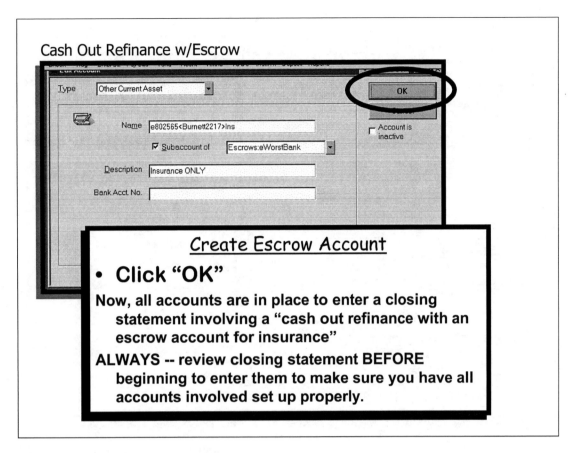

Cash Out Refinance w/Escrow

Type: Other Current Asset | OK

Name: e802565<Burnett2217>Ins
☑ Subaccount of: Escrows:eWorstBank
☐ Account is inactive
Description: Insurance ONLY
Bank Acct. No.

Create Escrow Account

- **Click "OK"**

Now, all accounts are in place to enter a closing statement involving a "cash out refinance with an escrow account for insurance"

ALWAYS -- review closing statement BEFORE beginning to enter them to make sure you have all accounts involved set up properly.

Finally select OK.

Review again, and ask yourself if all of the accounts involved are set up to complete the Cash Out Refinance with an Escrow account.

If you are confident you have done so, move on.

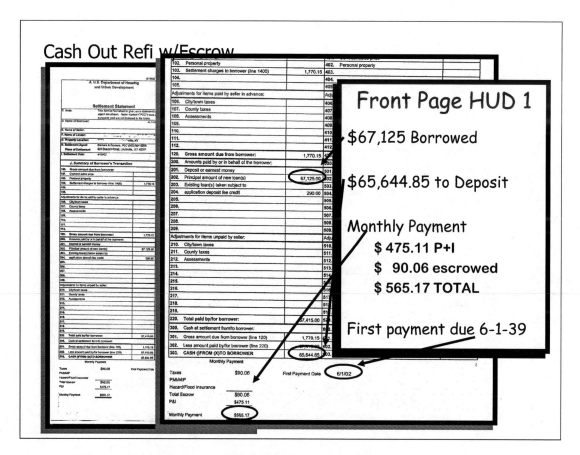

Cash Out Refi w/Escrow

Front Page HUD 1

$67,125 Borrowed

$65,644.85 to Deposit

Monthly Payment
- $ 475.11 P+I
- $ 90.06 escrowed
- $ 565.17 TOTAL

First payment due 6-1-39

The front page of the HUD 1

Make it easy on your CPA.

In the above example, you can see the amount borrowed, amount to deposit, along with the monthly payment information.

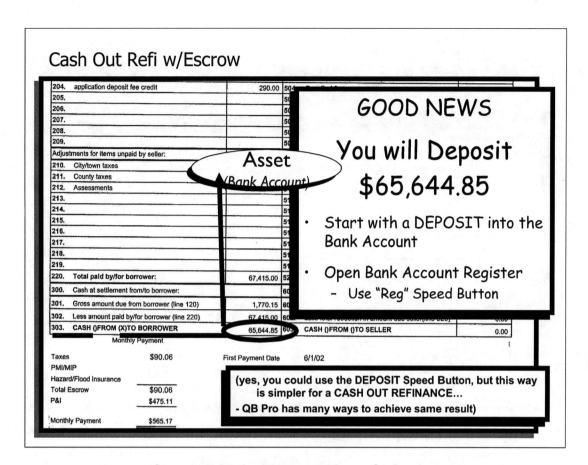

Cash Out Refi w/Escrow

204.	application deposit fee credit		290.00	504	
205.				50	
206.				50	
207.				50	
208.				50	
209.				50	

Adjustments for items unpaid by seller:

210.	City/town taxes			51	
211.	County taxes			51	
212.	Assessments			51	
213.				51	
214.				51	
215.				51	
216.				51	
217.				51	
218.				51	
219.				51	
220.	Total paid by/for borrower:		67,415.00	52	
300.	Cash at settlement from/to borrower:			60	
301.	Gross amount due from borrower (line 120)		1,770.15	60	
302.	Less amount paid by/for borrower (line 220)		67,415.00	60	
303.	CASH ()FROM (X)TO BORROWER		65,644.85	60	CASH ()FROM ()TO SELLER	0.00

Asset
(Bank Account)

Monthly Payment

Taxes	$90.06
PMI/MIP	
Hazard/Flood Insurance	
Total Escrow	$90.06
P&I	$475.11
Monthly Payment	$565.17

First Payment Date   6/1/02

GOOD NEWS

You will Deposit $65,644.85

- Start with a DEPOSIT into the Bank Account

- Open Bank Account Register
  - Use "Reg" Speed Button

(yes, you could use the DEPOSIT Speed Button, but this way is simpler for a CASH OUT REFINANCE...
- QB Pro has many ways to achieve same result)

Remember, REGARDLESS of the activity,

If you leave with money, START with a DEPOSIT

Tattoo the above backwards on your forehead so you can read it in the mirror.

Go the Bank account where the money will be deposited, and start there with a DEPOSIT.

Cash Out Refi w/Escrow

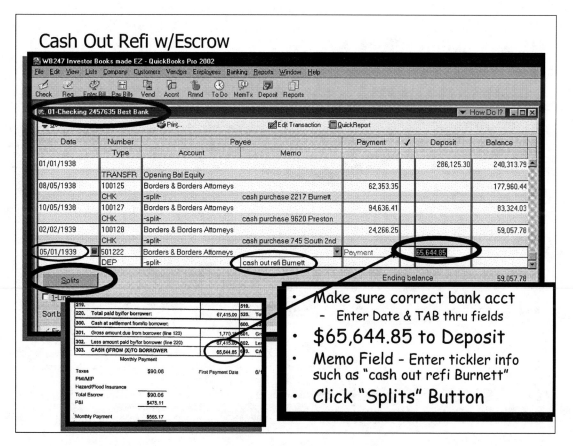

Check your top circled line making sure you are in the correct bank account.

TAB to the date field and enter proper date.

TAB to Deposit field and enter amount of Deposit.

TAB to MEMO field and briefly describe the transaction. For example, cash out refi of Burnett2217

TAB to or use your mouse and click on the SPLITS button.

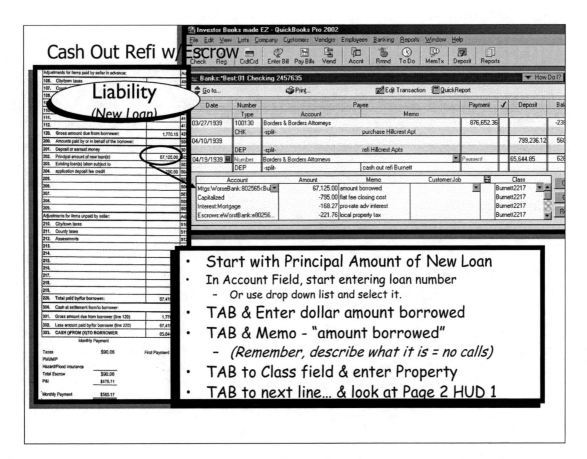

Cash Out Refi w/ Escrow

Liability (New Loan)

- Start with Principal Amount of New Loan
- In Account Field, start entering loan number
  - Or use drop down list and select it.
- TAB & Enter dollar amount borrowed
- TAB & Memo - "amount borrowed"
  - (Remember, describe what it is = no calls)
- TAB to Class field & enter Property
- TAB to next line... & look at Page 2 HUD 1

Remember your CPA and make it simple for them. Let's enter the amount borrowed first.

TAB to Account field and enter the new liability account you just created.

TAB to dollar amount and enter amount borrowed.

TAB to MEMO & enter Amount Borrowed.

TAB to CLASS and enter proper CLASS

TAB to next line and flip this page.

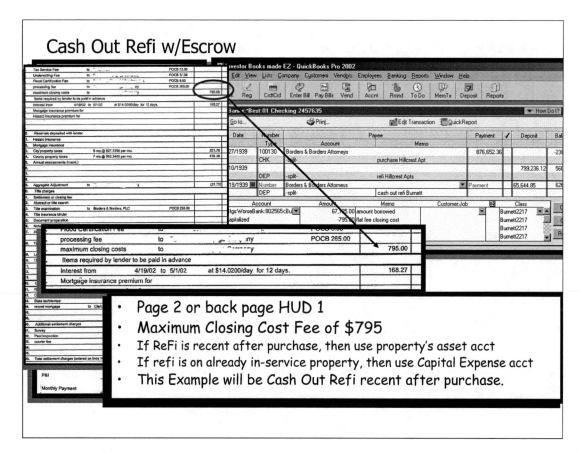

Cash Out Refi w/Escrow

- Page 2 or back page HUD 1
- Maximum Closing Cost Fee of $795
- If ReFi is recent after purchase, then use property's asset acct
- If refi is on already in-service property, then use Capital Expense acct
- This Example will be Cash Out Refi recent after purchase.

Look at the back page of your statement.

All of the fees associated with creating this loan are "capitalized expenses". Enter them one at a time using the Capitalized Expense account.

Do not confuse reserved funds held for future disbursement (lender setting up an escrow account for you)

TAB to MEMO field and describe each item as noted on the closing statement.

NOTE: pay attention to items paid outside of closing and are not directly involved in this transaction.

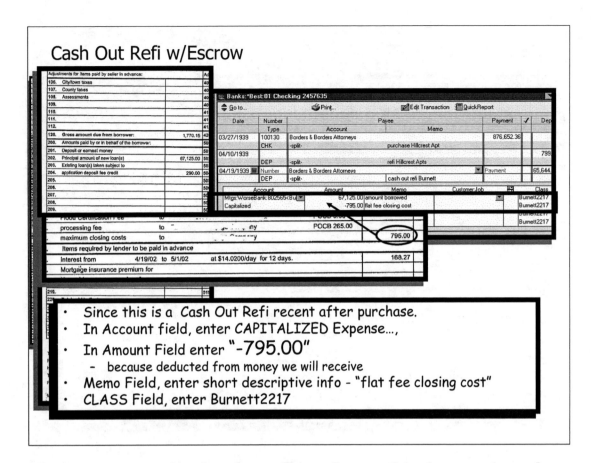

Cash Out Refi w/Escrow

- Since this is a Cash Out Refi recent after purchase.
- In Account field, enter CAPITALIZED Expense...,
- In Amount Field enter "-795.00"
  - because deducted from money we will receive
- Memo Field, enter short descriptive info - "flat fee closing cost"
- CLASS Field, enter Burnett2217

This example has a flat fee closing cost by the lender.

TAB to MEMO field and describe this line briefly, for example "FLAT FEE CLOSING COST"

Pay attention to the dollar amount field. In this example, you are starting with a deposit, so fees and expenses will be DEDUCTED from the money you borrowed – this simply means you place a MINUS sign in front of the dollar amount.

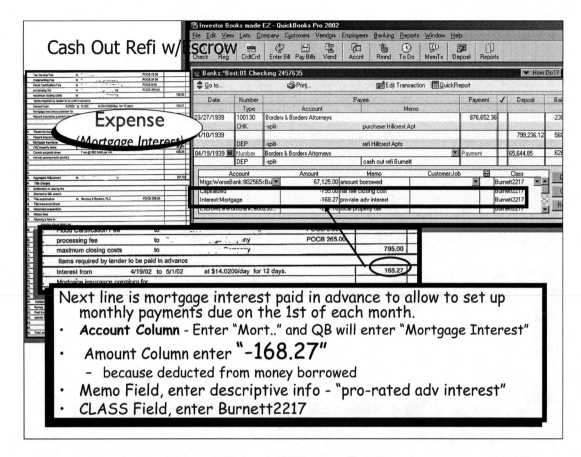

Cash Out Refi w/Escrow

Expense
(Mortgage Interest)

Next line is mortgage interest paid in advance to allow to set up monthly payments due on the 1st of each month.

- **Account Column** - Enter "Mort.." and QB will enter "Mortgage Interest"
- **Amount Column** enter **"-168.27"**
  - because deducted from money borrowed
- Memo Field, enter descriptive info - "pro-rated adv interest"
- CLASS Field, enter Burnett2217

Many lenders will collect some pro-rated interest in advance in order to get your loan payments set up for the 1st of each month. In these situations, you will be paying pro-rated MORTGAGE INTEREST in advance.

Again, this money will be DEDUCTED from the money you are borrowing and you will place a MINUS sign in front of the dollar amount.

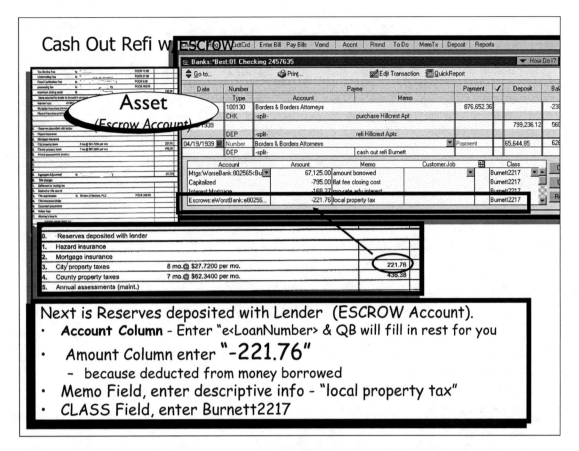

Cash Out Refi w/ ESCROW

Asset (Escrow Account)

Next is Reserves deposited with Lender (ESCROW Account).
- **Account Column** - Enter "e<LoanNumber>" & QB will fill in rest for you
- Amount Column enter **"-221.76"**
    - because deducted from money borrowed
- Memo Field, enter descriptive info - "local property tax"
- CLASS Field, enter Burnett2217

Lenders may set up an ESCROW account to hold YOUR MONEY to pay bills later. These are usually associated with Property Taxes, Insurance, Flood Insurance, etc. It can be set up for all or part, but either way it is still YOUR MONEY they are holding. It is NOT an expense.

Later in the year, you use this escrow account just like a bank account. Simply open the register for the escrow account involved and make a payment to the proper vendor for property taxes, insurance, etc.

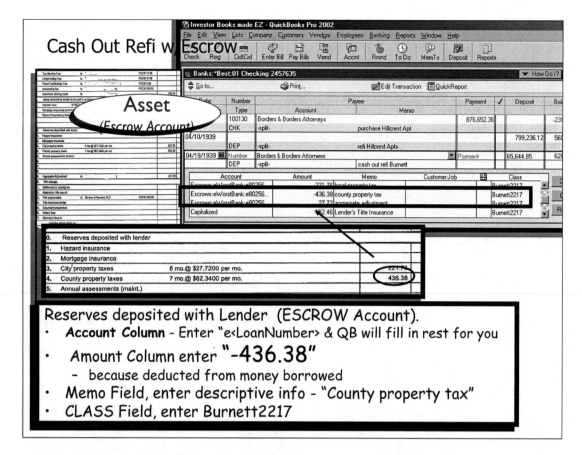

Cash Out Refi w Escrow

Reserves deposited with Lender (ESCROW Account).
- **Account Column** - Enter "e<LoanNumber> & QB will fill in rest for you
- Amount Column enter **"-436.38"**
  - because deducted from money borrowed
- Memo Field, enter descriptive info - "County property tax"
- CLASS Field, enter Burnett2217

When using an escrow account set up by the lender, you will use the escrow account involved to dump your "reserves held in advance" funds.

TAB to MEMO field and describe briefly (as noted above) what the funds are being held for future payment.

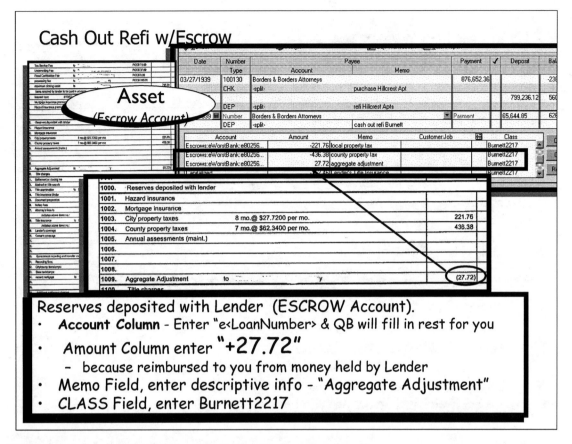

Cash Out Refi w/Escrow

Asset
(Escrow Account)

1000.	Reserves deposited with lender		
1001.	Hazard insurance		
1002.	Mortgage insurance		
1003.	City property taxes	8 mo.@ $27.7200 per mo.	221.76
1004.	County property taxes	7 mo.@ $62.3400 per mo.	436.38
1005.	Annual assessments (maint.)		
1006.			
1007.			
1008.			
1009.	Aggregate Adjustment	to ....y	(27.72)
1100.	Title charges		

Reserves deposited with Lender (ESCROW Account).
- **Account Column** - Enter "e<LoanNumber> & QB will fill in rest for you
- **Amount Column enter "+27.72"**
  - because reimbursed to you from money held by Lender
- Memo Field, enter descriptive info - "Aggregate Adjustment"
- CLASS Field, enter Burnett2217

This example used above is a real life closing statement.

Notice there is a line 1009 is titled AGGREGATE ADJUSTMENT. I do not have a clue why this is on there. In this example, this is not a big deal because it involves RESERVED FUNDS HELD IN ADVANCE. Again, this is an adjustment the lender made to how much of MY MONEY they are going to hold in advance for future disbursement.

Do NOT confuse this with an attitude of accepting everything on a closing statement. Review closing statements carefully and challenge anything you do not understand. If it is the least bit fuzzy, ASK QUESTIONS. The only dumb question is the one you never ask.

My point here is to stay focused on your objective.

THE OBJECTIVE IS ENTER THE ENTIRE CLOSING STATEMENT CORRECTLY SO YOU CAN PUT IT IN A FILING CABINET,

SET IT AND FORGET IT.

Make your closing statement entries EXACTLY as they appear on the real closing statement. If you stick with solid ground rule, You will NEVER have to haul closing statements to your tax preparer because the closing statement is right here!

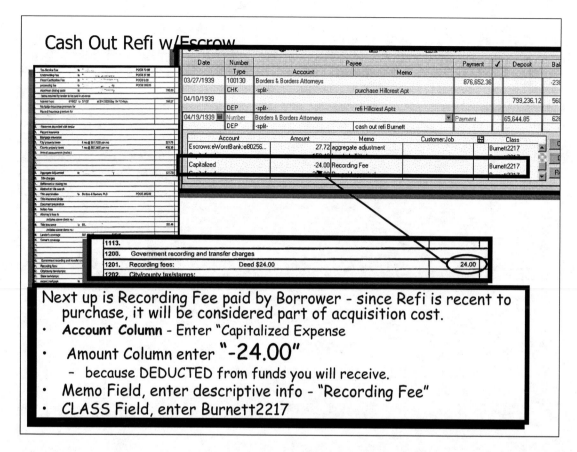

Next up is Recording Fee paid by Borrower - since Refi is recent to purchase, it will be considered part of acquisition cost.

- **Account Column** - Enter "Capitalized Expense
- Amount Column enter **"-24.00"**
  - because DEDUCTED from funds you will receive.
- Memo Field, enter descriptive info - "Recording Fee"
- CLASS Field, enter Burnett2217

Again, this is money DEDUCTED from the money you are borrowing.

Remember, you are making a deposit here, so you will place a minus sign in front of this dollar amount for the recording fee.

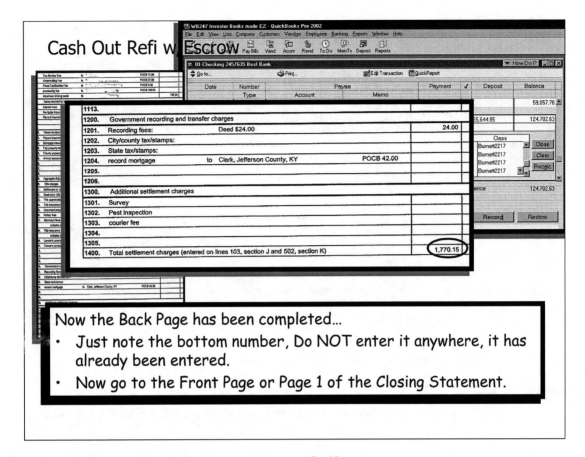

Review the back page carefully.

Make sure you have every dollar amount involved in this transaction entered properly.

Sometimes, in order to be thorough, many closing agents will note things PAID OUTSIDE OF CLOSING.. I have seen them flagged with POC or placed next to the column. They are simply nice to knows are NOT part of the transaction – so do NOT include them.

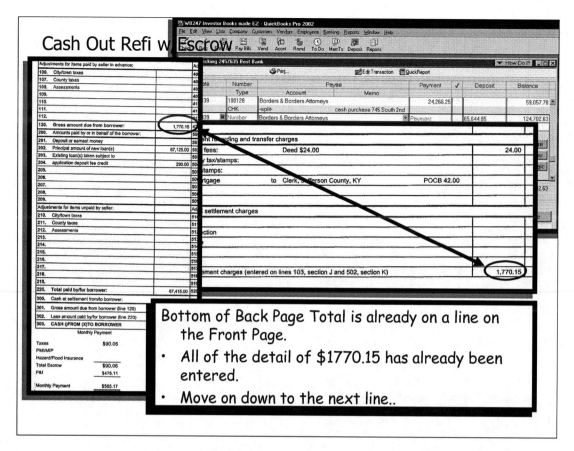

Cash Out Refi w Escrow

Bottom of Back Page Total is already on a line on the Front Page.
- All of the detail of $1770.15 has already been entered.
- Move on down to the next line..

Flip over to the front page and you will see the total from the bottom of the back page listed on the front page. Do not enter it again, this dollar amount on the front page is just a note of the subtotal involved of items listed on the back page.

Cash Out Refi w/Escrow

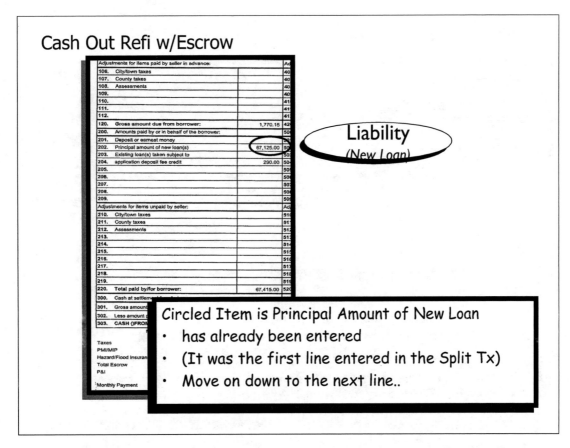

Adjustments for items paid by seller in advance:		Ac
106. City/town taxes		40
107. County taxes		40
108. Assessments		40
109.		40
110.		41
111.		41
112.		41
120. Gross amount due from borrower:	1,770.15	42
200. Amounts paid by or in behalf of the borrower:		50
201. Deposit or earnest money		50
202. Principal amount of new loan(s)	67,125.00	50
203. Existing loan(s) taken subject to		50
204. application deposit fee credit	290.00	50
205.		50
206.		50
207.		50
208.		50
209.		50
Adjustments for items unpaid by seller:		Ad
210. City/town taxes		51
211. County taxes		51
212. Assessments		51
213.		51
214.		51
215.		51
216.		51
217.		51
218.		51
219.		51
220. Total paid by/for borrower:	67,415.00	52
300. Cash at settlem...		
301. Gross amount		
302. Less amount		
303. CASH ()FROM		

Taxes
PMI/MIP
Hazard/Flood Insuran...
Total Escrow
P&I

Monthly Payment

Liability
(New Loan)

Circled Item is Principal Amount of New Loan
- has already been entered
- (It was the first line entered in the Split Tx)
- Move on down to the next line..

Remember, the objective here is to place this closing statement in the file cabinet forever.

As a User Friendly courtesy to our tax preparers, I always recommend making the top line of each closing statement in your Investor Books, the main transaction involved.

Simply put, if this closing statement involves a cash out refinance, then make the amount borrowed using your new liability account the very first line in your split transaction.

On the other hand, if you are purchasing a property, the first line would be using your new asset account with the purchase price. It really makes it simple for your tax preparer.

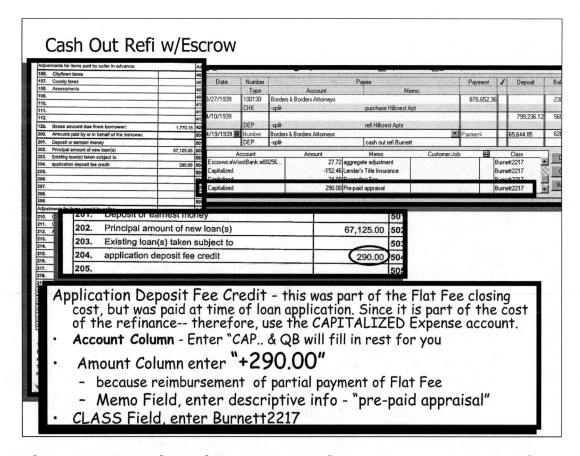

Cash Out Refi w/Escrow

Application Deposit Fee Credit - this was part of the Flat Fee closing cost, but was paid at time of loan application. Since it is part of the cost of the refinance-- therefore, use the CAPITALIZED Expense account.
- **Account Column** - Enter "CAP.. & QB will fill in rest for you
- Amount Column enter "**+290.00**"
  - because reimbursement of partial payment of Flat Fee
  - Memo Field, enter descriptive info - "pre-paid appraisal"
- CLASS Field, enter Burnett2217

The example above involves a step used many times with lenders.

The lender may require you to pay for an appraisal and / or credit report at the time of application. If these costs are included as part of a flat fee program, you will be reimbursed these funds on the closing statement.

155

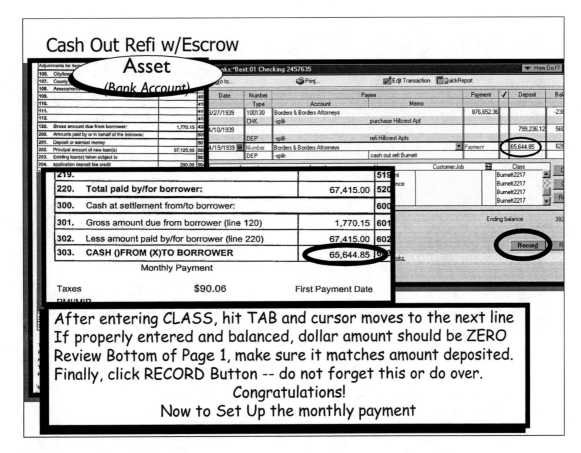

Cash Out Refi w/Escrow

Asset
(Bank Account)

After entering CLASS, hit TAB and cursor moves to the next line
If properly entered and balanced, dollar amount should be ZERO
Review Bottom of Page 1, make sure it matches amount deposited.
Finally, click RECORD Button -- do not forget this or do over.
Congratulations!
Now to Set Up the monthly payment

Almost done here,

A couple of things to check.

1.) Make sure the dollar amount to be deposited into your bank account MATCHES the dollar amount listed on the bottom of Page 1.

2.) YOU MUST HIT THE RECORD BUTTON to successfully complete entering this transaction!

Cash Out Refi w/Escrow – w/ Old Loan

If you have an existing loan(s) on this property you are refinancing, you will simply enter the dollar amount needed to pay off each loan and use the "MORTGAGE INTEREST" expense account.

Remember, out of all of the refinances I have done over the years, there has not been 1 time where their pay off has matched mine.

1.) If you are paying off and existing loan(s) with your refinance, as noted above, deduct from the money you are receiving, the amount needed to pay off the loan and use the "MORTGAGE INTEREST" expense account.

2.) After entering the closing statement, go to your Chart of Accounts, find the loan account that was just paid off, open the register and ZERO it out, DECREASE by the existing balance in the register using the PRINCIPAL PAID subaccount of your mortgage interest expense account.

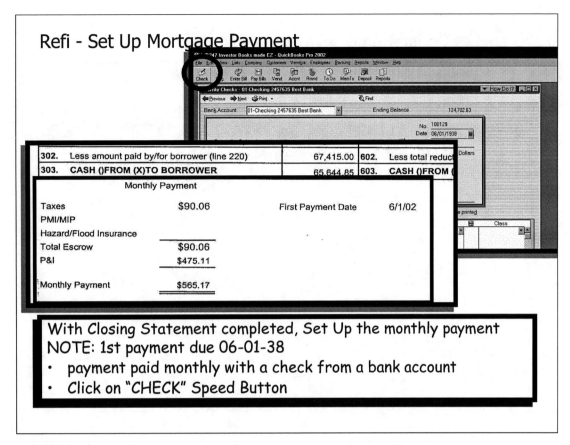

Refi - Set Up Mortgage Payment

	Monthly Payment			
Taxes	$90.06	First Payment Date	6/1/02
PMI/MIP			
Hazard/Flood Insurance			
Total Escrow	$90.06		
P&I	$475.11		
Monthly Payment	$565.17		

With Closing Statement completed, Set Up the monthly payment
NOTE: 1st payment due 06-01-38
- payment paid monthly with a check from a bank account
- Click on "CHECK" Speed Button

You have just completed the closing statement involving borrowing more money.

Most have monthly payments associated with the new loan.

If you are going to create a check for each monthly payment, this is where you would start.

Before you enter this check, let's look at why it is done in this manner.

Click on CREATE CHECK Speed Button and select the proper bank account.

NOTE

QuickBooks Pro® does NOT amortize loans.

(Use Quicken® 's powerful loan tracking feature for annual comparisons for both borrowing and loaning money)

Enter entire "PRINCIPAL & INTEREST" payment into the "MORTGAGE INTEREST" Expense account.

REASON:

- This allows the "Profit & Loss" Report by Class to reflect actual "cash flow" of each property.

If you edit your monthly memorized "split transaction" to enter the detail of the principal reduction along with the mortgage interest paid, ...

(you have too much time on your hands!)

Very cumbersome, this would require monthly "manual" editing of EACH & EVERY transaction

Time consuming, and defeats the purpose of setting up a system for the Aggressive Investor.

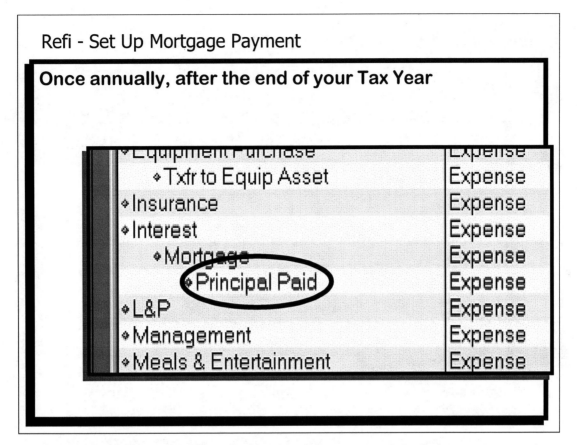

Refi - Set Up Mortgage Payment

Once annually, after the end of your Tax Year

Equipment Purchase	Expense
◆ Txfr to Equip Asset	Expense
◆ Insurance	Expense
◆ Interest	Expense
◆ Mortgage	Expense
◆ Principal Paid	Expense
◆ L&P	Expense
◆ Management	Expense
◆ Meals & Entertainment	Expense

Once annually (after the end of your Tax Year)
- Open the Liability Account Register for the loan involved
- Enter the last day of your Tax Year (usually December 31)
- Payee can be left blank
- Dollar Amount "decrease" field, -- enter the dollar amount of principal reduction for the year.
>   -Compare to 1098's received & Quicken® loan tracking
- ACCOUNT field: use "Principal PAID"
- MEMO field: enter "1098=<dollar amount>"
>   (Allows your CPA to see 1098 data without paper)
- Remember to enter "CLASS"

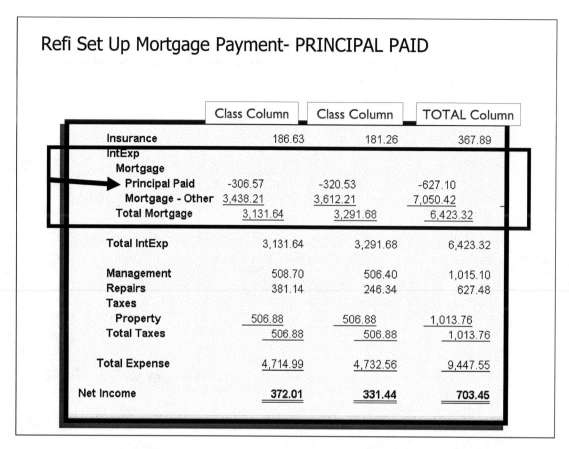

Refi Set Up Mortgage Payment- PRINCIPAL PAID

	Class Column	Class Column	TOTAL Column
Insurance	186.63	181.26	367.89
IntExp			
Mortgage			
Principal Paid	-306.57	-320.53	-627.10
Mortgage - Other	3,438.21	3,612.21	7,050.42
Total Mortgage	3,131.64	3,291.68	6,423.32
Total IntExp	3,131.64	3,291.68	6,423.32
Management	508.70	506.40	1,015.10
Repairs	381.14	246.34	627.48
Taxes			
Property	506.88	506.88	1,013.76
Total Taxes	506.88	506.88	1,013.76
Total Expense	4,714.99	4,732.56	9,447.55
Net Income	372.01	331.44	703.45

This is powerful.

Profit and Loss Report will now show how much was spent:

- total on Mortgage Payments

- Principal Paid for the year

- Mortgage Interest paid for the year

Keep in mind, QB Pro's fantastic report feature shows this information by each property, each LLC and total of ALL, with just a couple of clicks!! Amazing.

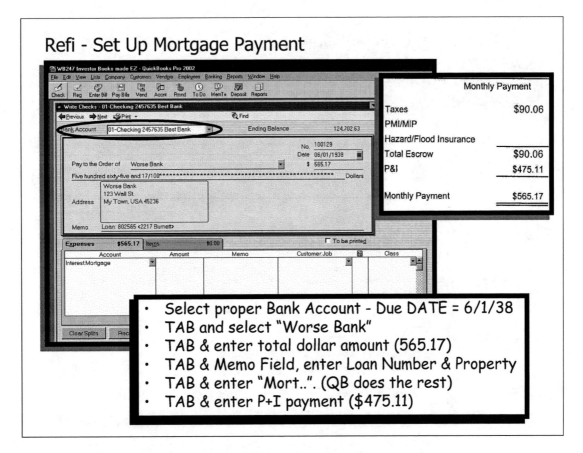

Click CREATE CHECK speed button

- Select proper Bank Account - Due DATE = 6/1/38
- TAB and select "Worse Bank"
- TAB & enter total dollar amount (565.17)
- TAB & Memo Field, enter Loan Number & Property
- TAB & enter "Mort..". (QB does the rest)
- TAB & enter P+I payment ($475.11)

NOTE: MEMO FIELD on the CHECK, briefly describe what the payment is for and include the LOAN NUMBER and property address.

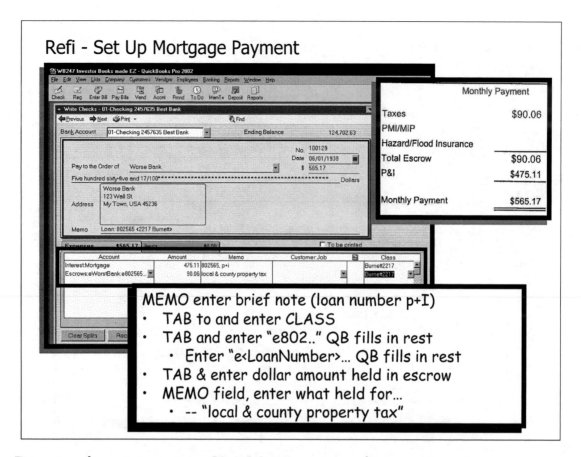

Refi - Set Up Mortgage Payment

MEMO enter brief note (loan number p+I)
- TAB to and enter CLASS
- TAB and enter "e802.." QB fills in rest
  - Enter "e<LoanNumber>... QB fills in rest
- TAB & enter dollar amount held in escrow
- MEMO field, enter what held for...
  - -- "local & county property tax"

Remember to enter CLASS on every line on every transaction in Investor Books.

If an escrow account is involved, use the ESCROW account, not the expense the funds are being held for. Remember, escrow account involve YOUR MONEY the lender is holding for future payment of expenses.

IMPORTANT

MAKE SURE **TO BE PRINTED** BOX IS CHECKED, the check could be entered automatically in your register using the next sequential number, with no notice to you.

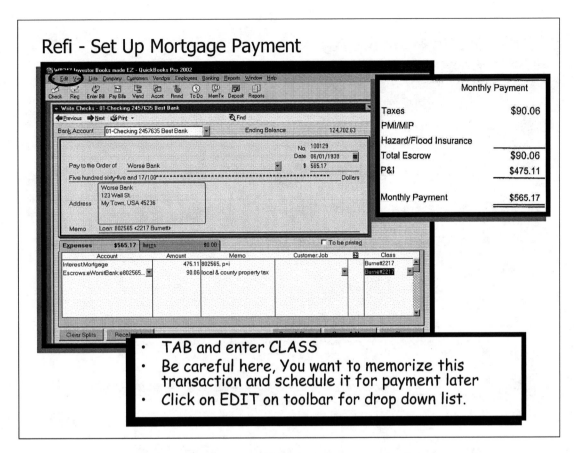

Refi - Set Up Mortgage Payment

	Monthly Payment
Taxes	$90.06
PMI/MIP	
Hazard/Flood Insurance	
Total Escrow	$90.06
P&I	$475.11
Monthly Payment	$565.17

- TAB and enter CLASS
- Be careful here, You want to memorize this transaction and schedule it for payment later
- Click on EDIT on toolbar for drop down list.

Review your check, if you agree it looks proper, you must now MEMORIZE IT to get it in your automated system.

You MUST CREATE a transaction BEFORE you can memorize it.

Click on EDIT on toolbar, a drop down list will appear.

Refi - Set Up Mortgage Payment

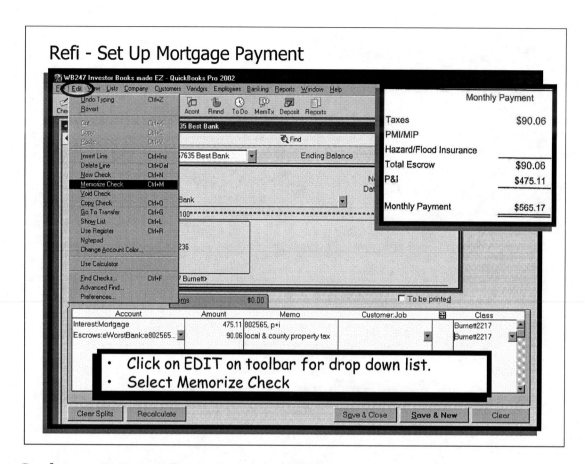

Select MEMORIZE CHECK.

Pretty simple, huh?

Refi - Set Up Mortgage Payment

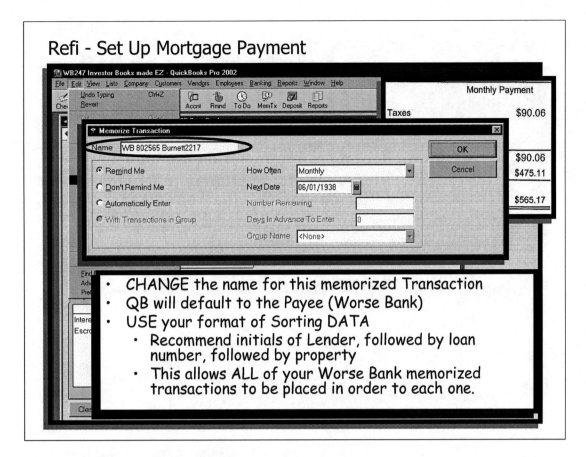

PAY ATTENTION HERE.

This window appears and the name for this check to memorize will default to the name of the PAYEE (vendor).

Imagine having 30 mortgage payments to Worse Bank. They would all be named Worse Bank and cause a mess in your list of memorized transactions. Therefore, let's edit the name of this memorized check to make sense for you.

Name the memorized Check as:

"WrstBnk<LoanNumber>Property"

Refi - Set Up Mortgage Payment

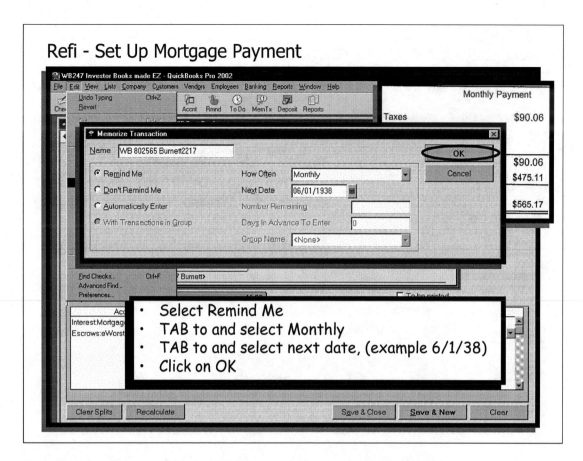

- Select Remind Me
- TAB to and select Monthly
- TAB to and select next date, (example 6/1/38)
- Click on OK

TAB thru and follow the easy steps.

If your payment is monthly, select monthly.

In the DATE DUE field enter the real date the payment is actually due.

Do NOT try to set up advanced dates here. This is already set up for you in Investor Books.

If you set this payment to be due on the 1st of next month, Investor Books will automatically remind you 10 DAYS in advance this payment is due.

Refi - Set Up Mortgage Payment

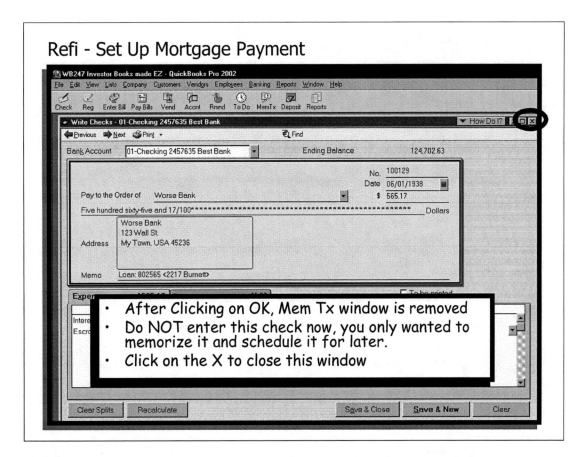

After you have successfully CREATE the check and memorized it, click on the MEM TX Speed Button to see if your memorized transaction has been placed on the list.

Once done, click on the X in the create check window. Remember, you just created a check to be paid somewhere in the future, odds are, you do not want to actually make a payment right now. Therefore, you must cancel this check and not enter it in your check book register.

Refi - Set Up Mortgage Payment

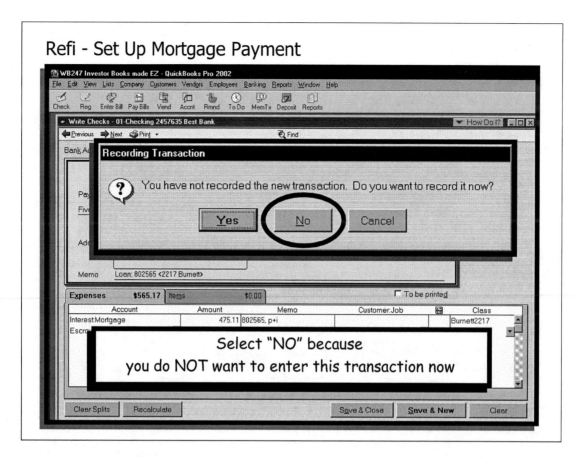

After hitting the X, this window will appear.

Again, assuming you do not want to record this transaction at this time, answer the question and select NO.

Refi - Set Up Mortgage Payment for Auto Pay

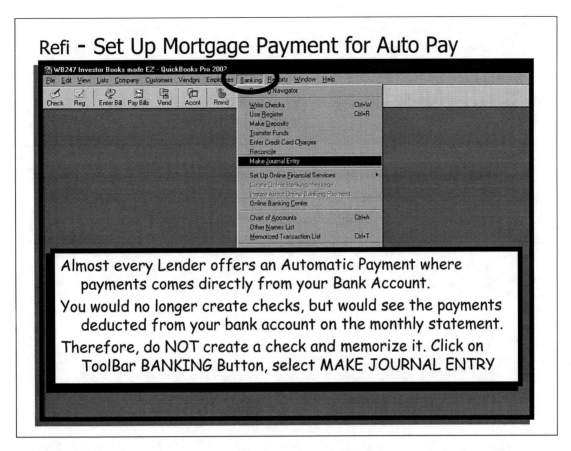

Almost every Lender offers an Automatic Payment where payments comes directly from your Bank Account.

You would no longer create checks, but would see the payments deducted from your bank account on the monthly statement.

Therefore, do NOT create a check and memorize it. Click on ToolBar BANKING Button, select MAKE JOURNAL ENTRY

If you have payments automatically deducted from a bank account, you will set these up here.

On the TOOL BAR click on BANKING.

Select JOURNAL ENTRY.

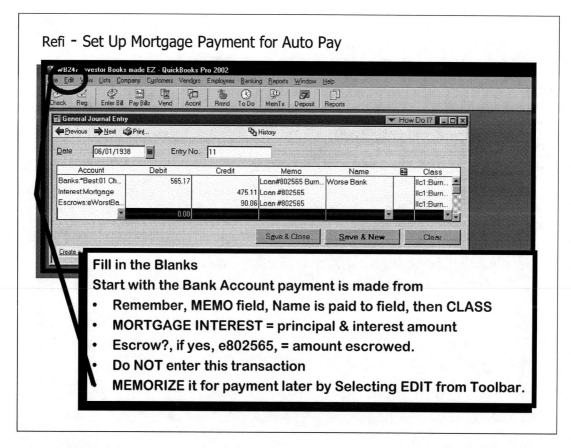

Refi - Set Up Mortgage Payment for Auto Pay

I do not like the JOURNAL ENTRY window because of the debit and credit words. I do not understand them and don't want to.

Here is my version of this transaction... (Remember, the post office and the walls of boxes. The journal entry window is like giving instructions to the little man in the middle of the room. Go to this bank account and pull out X amount of money. Then place X amount into this account, and X amount in to that account.)

Again, you must always use classes.

When set up properly, follow the proper procedures to MEMORIZE this transaction.

On the TOOL BAR, click EDIT, select MEMORIZE and rename it properly to make sense to you when you are reading your list of memorized transactions.

"WrsBnk<LoanNumber>Property"

Selling – Closing Statements

Regardless of the activity...

If You BRING Money
You Start with a Check

If You Get Money
You Start with a DEPOSIT

MEMORIZE these phrases.

It will always keep you on track and allow you to start in the right place.

Following this rule will make it EASY for you to understand.

Closing Statement- Selling has 3 Steps

Step 1 - enter closing statement
Step 2 - What are you selling?
- **a Fixed Asset Acct.**
- You will no longer own it
- Must ZERO out that Fixed Asset
- You can NOT sell it & still own it.

STEP 2 is hard to remember when You are busy and cranking.

STEP 3 – Edit the CLASS

STEP 2 believe it or not, is probably one of the hardest steps to remember. (just ask any CPA, accountant, etc. who reviews books kept by the investor.)

You can not sell your Asset and still own it.

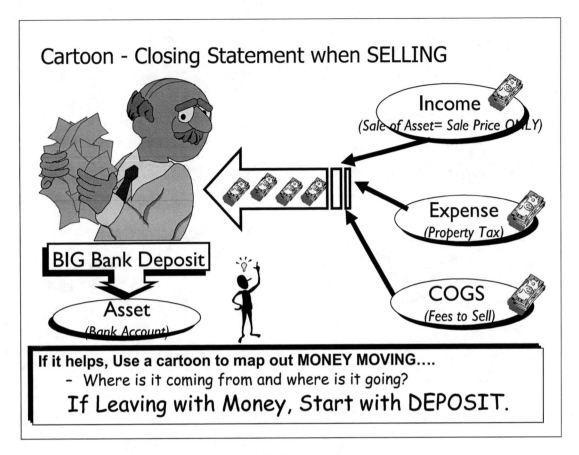

Cartoons help me to figure out what is going on with the closing statement.

If you are leaving with MONEY, you will start with a bank deposit and work backwards.

The deposit you make is the result of all of the other stuff on the right.

The listed example is a simple cash sale with pro-rated property taxes and the fees involved to sell your asset.

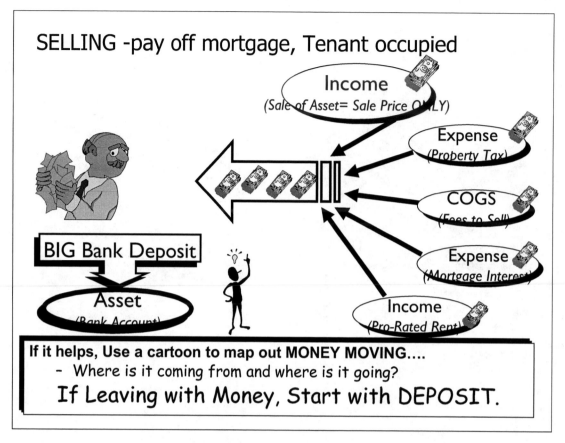

Here again, just add additional variables if they are involved in your transaction.

Such things:

- Tenant occupied? Pro-rated rent

       use RENT INCOME account

- Property Taxes?

       use TAX:PROPERTY expense account

- pay off existing mortgages?

       use INTEREST:MORTGAGE expense account

       (the liability account itself will be zero'd out using the interest:mortgage:principal paid expense account)

- anything else involved.

Draw it out if needed, you MUST understand what is going on BEFORE you start.

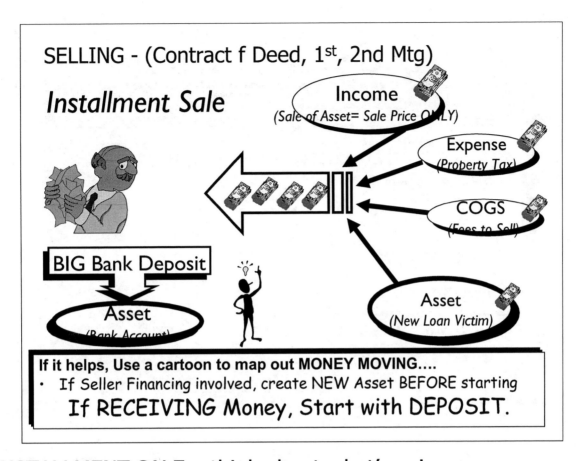

INSTALLMENT SALE – think about what's going on.

You are selling an asset and **YOU are financing** all or part of your buyer's funds needed to make the purchase.

Your closing statement could be scribbled on paper towel, but scribble out something that makes sense to you.

When you finance part of your buyer funds needed, you are actually LOANING them money.

Your buyer has become an asset for You.

Your Buyer OWES YOU MONEY.

You must create a new ASSET account for your victim.

Do this BEFORE you start on the closing statement.

Selling Step 1 - Cash Deal

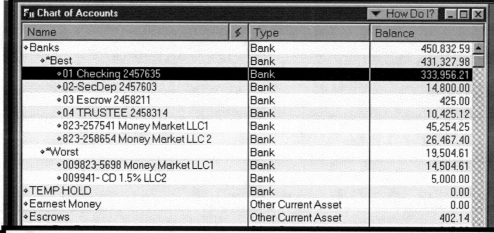

Name	$	Type	Balance
◆Banks		Bank	450,832.59
◆*Best		Bank	431,327.98
◆01 Checking 2457635		Bank	333,956.21
◆02-SecDep 2457603		Bank	14,800.00
◆03 Escrow 2458211		Bank	425.00
◆04 TRUSTEE 2458314		Bank	10,425.12
◆823-257541 Money Market LLC1		Bank	45,254.25
◆823-258654 Money Market LLC 2		Bank	26,467.40
◆*Worst		Bank	19,504.61
◆009823-5698 Money Market LLC1		Bank	14,504.61
◆009941- CD 1.5% LLC2		Bank	5,000.00
◆TEMP HOLD		Bank	0.00
◆Earnest Money		Other Current Asset	0.00
◆Escrows		Other Current Asset	402.14

Receiving Money at Closing = Start with Bank Deposit
- From Chart of Accounts
- Double click Bank Account to deposit money

SELLING simple cash deal.

You will be receiving money and making a bank deposit. GOOD PLACE TO START.

Go to bank account and open the register.

Selling Step 1 - Cash Deal

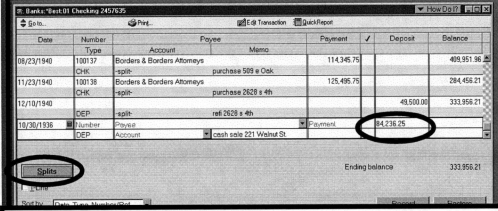

Date	Number	Payee		Payment	✓	Deposit	Balance
	Type	Account	Memo				
08/23/1940	100137	Borders & Borders Attorneys		114,345.75			409,951.96
	CHK	-split-	purchase 509 e Oak				
11/23/1940	100138	Borders & Borders Attorneys		125,495.75			284,456.21
	CHK	-split-	purchase 2628 s 4th				
12/10/1940						49,500.00	333,956.21
	DEP	-split-	refi 2628 s 4th				
10/30/1936	Number	Payee		Payment		84,236.25	
	DEP	Account	cash sale 221 Walnut St.				

Splits

Ending balance   333,956.21

Sort by

Cursor defaults to Date field, enter correct date
- **TAB to DEPOSIT & enter Receive Money**
- **TAB to MEMO & enter brief description**
- **Select SPLITS Button to start closing statement**

TAB thru enter the proper amounts and detail in each field.

MEMO field, pay attention, briefly describe the transaction so it makes sense as you view your register. Do not leave it blank.

In this example, the MEMO field would read SALE of Property Address.

Click on SPLITS button and enter the rest of your closing statement.

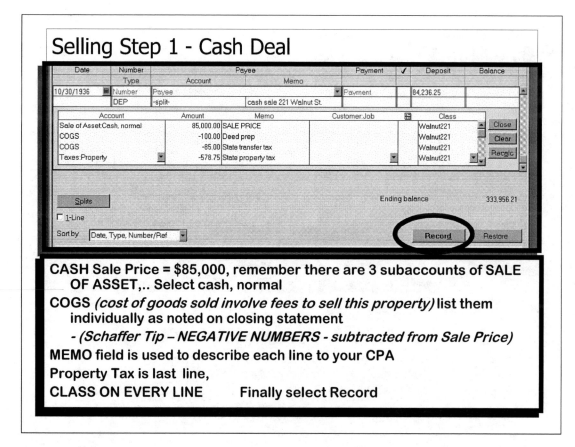

Selling Step 1 - Cash Deal

Date	Number	Payee		Payment	✓	Deposit	Balance
	Type	Account	Memo				
10/30/1936	Number	Payee		Payment		84,236.25	
	DEP	-split-	cash sale 221 Walnut St.				

Account	Amount	Memo	Customer:Job		Class	
Sale of Asset:Cash, normal	85,000.00	SALE PRICE			Walnut221	Close
COGS	-100.00	Deed prep			Walnut221	Clear
COGS	-85.00	State transfer tax			Walnut221	Recalc
Taxes:Property	-578.75	State property tax			Walnut221	

Splits

☐ 1-Line

Sort by   Date, Type, Number/Ref

Ending balance   333,956.21

Record   Restore

CASH Sale Price = $85,000, remember there are 3 subaccounts of SALE OF ASSET,.. Select cash, normal

COGS *(cost of goods sold involve fees to sell this property)* list them individually as noted on closing statement

- *(Schaffer Tip – NEGATIVE NUMBERS - subtracted from Sale Price)*

MEMO field is used to describe each line to your CPA

Property Tax is last line,

CLASS ON EVERY LINE   Finally select Record

SALE OF ASSET has 3 sub-accounts. There are only 3 ways to sell your real estate.

    1.) Normal, cash, traditional

    2.) INSTALLMENT SALES

    3.) 1031 Tax Deferred Exchange

Only the actual Sale Price is used in the SALE OF ASSET account. Remember those 1099's you receive at the closing? They list the sale price as income and it is reported to the IRS so let's set the stage to make sure the SALE OF ASSET income account matches your 1099 the IRS will receive.

All of the fees involved with selling your real estate (asset) will use the COST OF GOODS SOLD account allowing your SALE OF ASSET income account to be sacred and not touched.

Selling - Step 2 for Every Sale

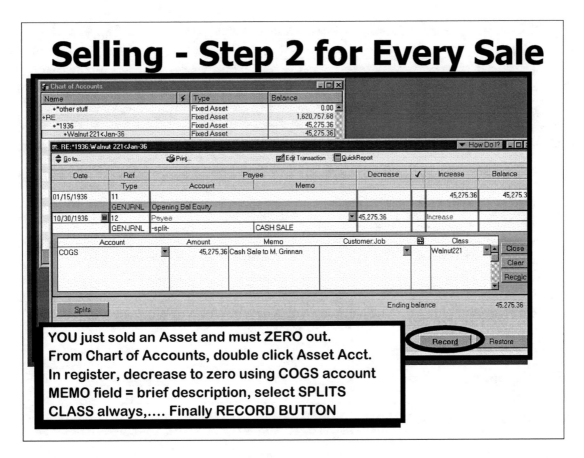

YOU just sold an Asset and must ZERO out.
From Chart of Accounts, double click Asset Acct.
In register, decrease to zero using COGS account
MEMO field = brief description, select SPLITS
CLASS always,.... Finally RECORD BUTTON

This is hard to remember.

You just SOLD an Asset.

You no longer own it.

Go to the Register for the sold asset.

TAB thru all fields and ZERO out the balance using the COST OF (your asset) GOODS SOLD account.

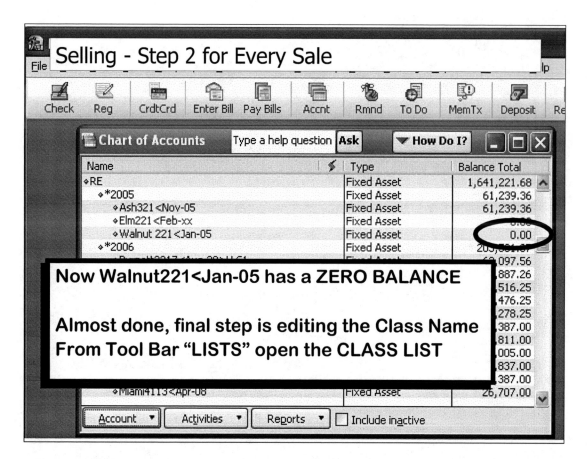

Selling - Step 2 for Every Sale

Chart of Accounts

Name	Type	Balance Total
◆RE	Fixed Asset	1,641,221.68
◆*2005	Fixed Asset	61,239.36
◆Ash321<Nov-05	Fixed Asset	61,239.36
◆Elm221<Feb-xx	Fixed Asset	
◆Walnut 221<Jan-05	Fixed Asset	0.00
◆*2006	Fixed Asset	

> **Now Walnut221<Jan-05 has a ZERO BALANCE**
>
> **Almost done, final step is editing the Class Name**
> **From Tool Bar "LISTS" open the CLASS LIST**

| ◆Miami4113<Apr-08 | Fixed Asset | 26,707.00 |

You will see in your chart of accounts, this asset will now have a balance of ZERO because you SOLD it.

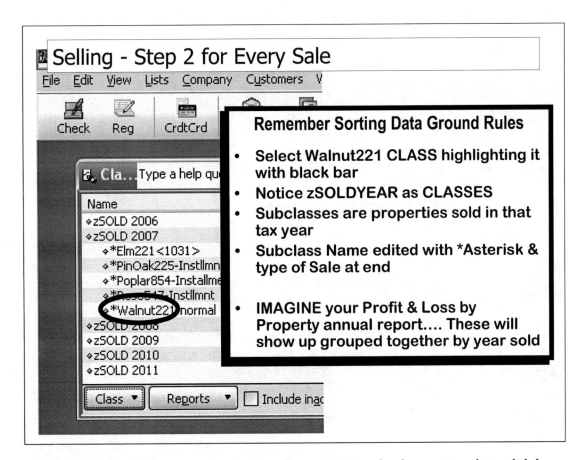

Selling - Step 2 for Every Sale

File   Edit   View   Lists   Company   Customers   V

Check   Reg   CrdtCrd

Cla.. Type a help qu

Name
◊zSOLD 2006
◊zSOLD 2007
  ◊*Elm221<1031>
  ◊*PinOak225-Instllmn
  ◊*Poplar854-Installme
  ◊*R___547-Instllmnt
  ◊*Walnut221 normal
◊zSOLD 2008
◊zSOLD 2009
◊zSOLD 2010
◊zSOLD 2011

Class ▼   Reports ▼   ☐ Include inac

Remember Sorting Data Ground Rules

- **Select Walnut221 CLASS highlighting it with black bar**
- **Notice zSOLDYEAR as CLASSES**
- **Subclasses are properties sold in that tax year**
- **Subclass Name edited with *Asterisk & type of Sale at end**

- **IMAGINE your Profit & Loss by Property annual report…. These will show up grouped together by year sold**

With selling this asset, another critical change should be completed now.

From the TOOL BAR, click on LISTS and select CLASS.

Select the property just sold, click on the class button, and select EDIT.

Place an *asterisk in front and make it a subclass of the year sold. *(If you sold this property using the Installment Sales method, you will be reporting income interest monthly and will be using this class every month; therefore, do not place an *asterisk in front of the class name.)*

This becomes important at the end of the year by allowing all properties sold by year to be grouped together at the end of your Profit and Loss Report.

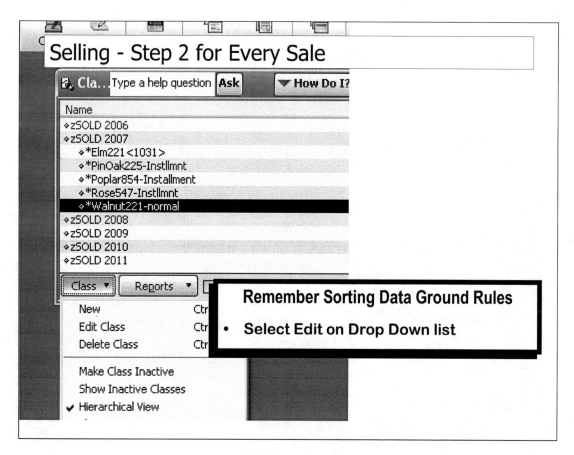

Notice the name of this property (CLASS) is edited with an *asterisk in front (to prevent it from being used easily)

The type of sale (normal, installment, 1031) should be listed after the name of the property. This becomes very useful on the Profit and Loss report.

Remember to make it a sub class of the year sold and click on OK

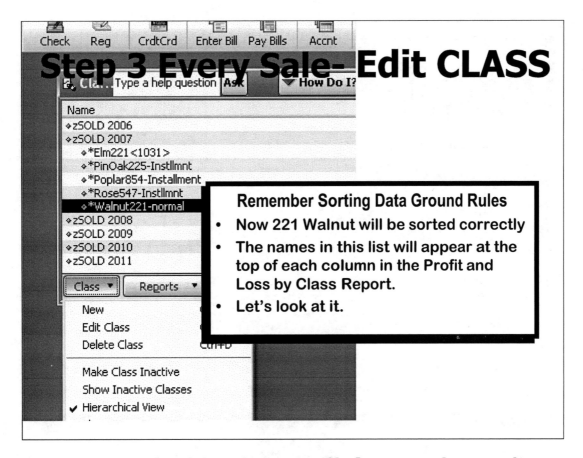

Step 3 Every Sale- Edit CLASS

You will see the class will fit neatly in the list by the year sold and you can easily see what kind of sale occurred.

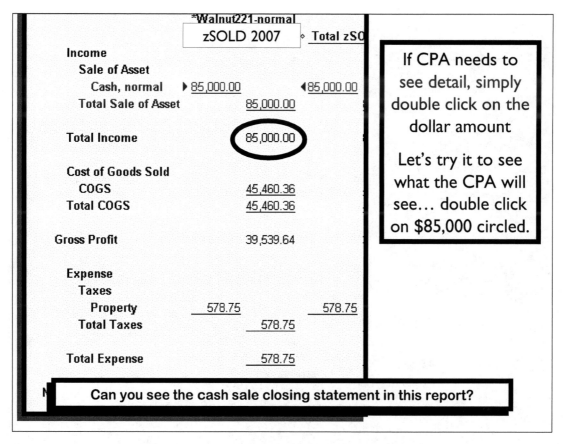

This is an example of your Profit and Loss report for the year.

The numbers on this report are used to prepare taxes.

You can immediately identify properties sold, by year, type of sale, etc.

If you, your CPA or accountant wants to see the detail, simply move the cursor over any dollar amount, it will change to a magnifying glass and double click your way all the back.

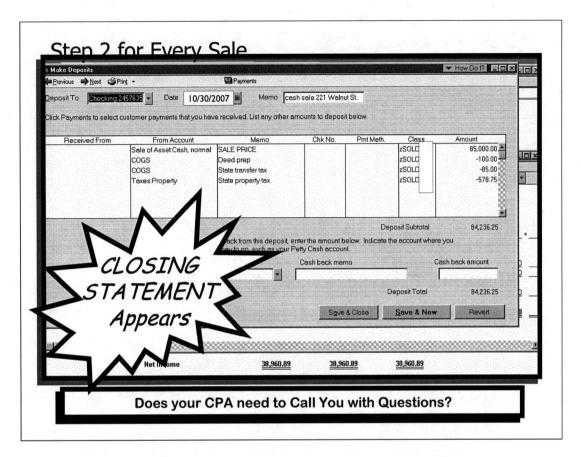

Step 2 for Every Sale

QB will take you right to the closing statement you entered.

This is what your CPA, accountant, or bookkeeper can do instead of hauling closing statements and receipts to them.

Teach them how to double click their way to the detail and closing statements.

If your tax preparer refuses to use QB, get a different one.

Cash Deal, Pay Off Mortgage

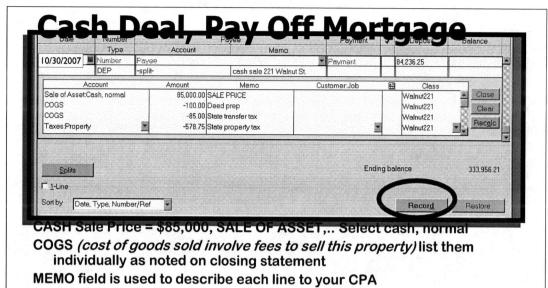

CASH Sale Price = $85,000, SALE OF ASSET,.. Select cash, normal

COGS *(cost of goods sold involve fees to sell this property)* list them
   individually as noted on closing statement

MEMO field is used to describe each line to your CPA

Property Tax is last line,

CLASS ON EVERY LINE

Enter *"Mortgage:Interest"* & enter pay off amount & CLASS

   Finally select Record

STEP 2 – go to Liability Account paid off & Zero out decreasing using the
   PrincipalPaid subaccount of Mortgage Interest.

   Finally delete the memorized transaction, you just PAID IT OFF.

Cash or Normal Traditional Sale AND paying off your 1st mortgage loan
Follow the steps above.

Always review the payoff amount from the lender who will be getting
paid in full. They do make mistakes. Try to get a copy of your closing
statement FAXED to you before the closing.

Enter the closing statement as normal, and enter the payoff amount to
the lender using the **Mortgage Interest** expense account. The lender's
payoff and your balance almost never matches... but it should be real
close.

2 Additional Steps:

1.) Go to the Liability Account just paid off and decrease it to ZERO
using the **PRINCIPAL paid** account.

2.) MEMORIZED TRANSACTION – this loan is PAID OFF, STOP IT NOW!
If you have automatic payments from one of your bank accounts, call
your banker and STOP IT NOW. No one will do it for you. And make
inactive or delete this memorized transaction from your list of
memorized transactions

Step 1 - Installment SALE

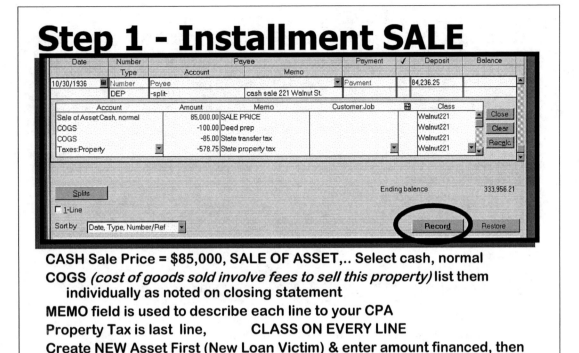

CASH Sale Price = $85,000, SALE OF ASSET,.. Select cash, normal

COGS *(cost of goods sold involve fees to sell this property)* list them individually as noted on closing statement

MEMO field is used to describe each line to your CPA

Property Tax is last line,   CLASS ON EVERY LINE

Create NEW Asset First (New Loan Victim) & enter amount financed, then enter CLASS

Finally select Record

Selling INSTALLMENT SALE. Again, if a cartoon helps, use it.

You must create a new ASSET for your new loan victim BEFORE you begin with the transaction.

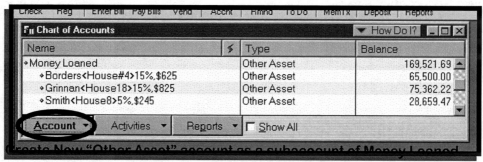

SALE Step 1 - Installment SALE - new asset acct

Name	〽	Type	Balance
◆ Money Loaned		Other Asset	169,521.69
◆ Borders<House#4>15%,$625		Other Asset	65,500.00
◆ Grinnan<House18>15%,$825		Other Asset	75,362.22
◆ Smith<House8>5%,$245		Other Asset	28,659.47

Account ▾ Activities ▾ Reports ▾ ☐ Show All

- Last Name of Borrower is recommend for EZ Fast find in QB Pro
- Do NOT enter a dollar amount when setting this up
- You will enter the dollar amount when entering the closing statement.

NOTE: do NOT try to memorize payments from loan customers here. THEY PAY LATE and BOUNCE CHECKS. Track all of their stuff in Tenant Tracking.

- When making deposits from Loan Customers, use the INCOME INTEREST for all payments received.
- At the end of the year, (after late charges, NSF, etc,) use the subaccount of INCOME INTEREST to reduce their balance owed.

Follow the instructions above to create a new OTHER ASSET for your new loan victim.

NEVER set up memorized transaction for payments you EXPECT to receive.

Although a nice thought it is DANGEROUS. They can be late and bounce checks. Report income as you receive it. Do not schedule income.

Installment SALE - year end report result

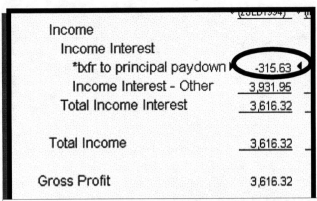

Income	
Income Interest	
*txfr to principal paydown	-315.63
Income Interest - Other	3,931.95
Total Income Interest	3,616.32
Total Income	3,616.32
Gross Profit	3,616.32

- Actual Profit and Loss Report for property sold using Installment Sale.
- Notice $3,931.95 actually received and deposited
- After the end of the year, an entry was made into the Money Loaned subaccount for Buyer decreasing their balanced owed by $315.63
- Using the subaccount, you can see total received, amount reduced, and net income of Income Interest from this Installment Sale.
- This happens every year, FYI, you could simply change the date range on the report and see results for several years combined.

As you receive payments from your loan victim, report all income into the INCOME INTEREST account.

Just like mortgage interest when you make mortgage payments, at the end of the year, you will make one entry in their asset account of the amount of principal paid down on their loan adjusting the balance they owe you.

Surprisingly, with late charges, bounced checks, and others, there may be a very small amount of principal paid. The point here is do not try to do it monthly.

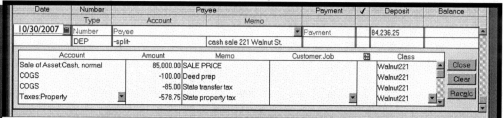

SALE Step 1 - w/ tenant, & more etc.

Date	Number		Payee		Payment	✓	Deposit	Balance
	Type	Account		Memo				
10/30/2007	Number	Payee			Payment		84,236.25	
	DEP	-split-		cash sale 221 Walnut St.				

Account	Amount	Memo	Customer:Job		Class	
Sale of Asset:Cash, normal	85,000.00	SALE PRICE			Walnut221	Close
COGS	-100.00	Deed prep			Walnut221	Clear
COGS	-85.00	State transfer tax			Walnut221	Recalc
Taxes:Property	-578.75	State property tax			Walnut221	

Many things can be involved with CLOSING STATEMENTS

Look at how many lines are on the form. Some folks try to use every line.

Whatever else is involved, just slow down, use the cartoon if needed and sort through the mess.

If it is Tenant occupied and rents will be pro-rated, then use the RENT INCOME account.

Entering a closing statement transaction into QB Pro can be simple by breaking it down to each line item.

If you have a lengthy closing statement with many line items, your closing statement entry could be over 20 lines.

When SELLING KEEP SALE PRICE BY ITSELF IN SALE OF ASSET

All other Fees involved with pulling off the sale go to COGS.

Adding more variables to the closing statement.

If tenants are involved with pro-rated rents, use the RENT INCOME account.

Jot it down if it helps you to sort it out.

ESCROWS - paying Taxes & Insurance

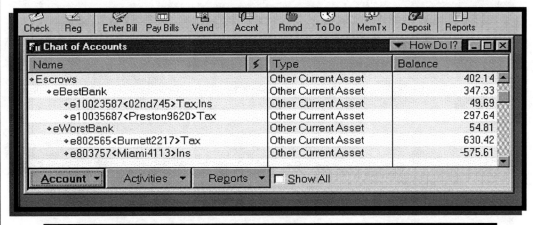

Name	⚡	Type	Balance
◆Escrows		Other Current Asset	402.14
◆eBestBank		Other Current Asset	347.33
◆e10023587<02nd745>Tax,Ins		Other Current Asset	49.69
◆e10035687<Preston9620>Tax		Other Current Asset	297.64
◆eWorstBank		Other Current Asset	54.81
◆e802565<Burnett2217>Tax		Other Current Asset	630.42
◆e803757<Miami4113>Ins		Other Current Asset	-575.61

See how your money is sorted by each Escrow account, by each Lender, and by all Escrows.
Powerful.
THIS IS YOUR MONEY until it gets spent.

YOUR money, held by Lender to pay Taxes and/or Insurance

When you receive notice of bill to paid from escrowed funds, simply double click on the escrow involved, and use it like a bank checkbook register.

I recommend requesting the Lender to cancel escrowed funds... very cumbersome as far as reconciling annually.

Imagine a 30yr fixed loan with P+I is constant.

Because of escrowed funds, payment will change annually.

If you have many, especially with EFT, Lender will screw up.

RETURNED CHECKS

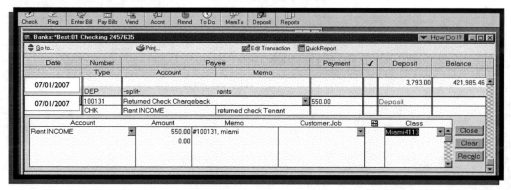

Notice the VENDOR or payee NAME, it is set up for you

RETURNED CHECK CHARGEBACK

Set up as a Vendor, RETURNED CHECK CHARGEBACK, use it in the payee field.

Open the register for the bank account involved.

Determine what the Returned check is for/from - If Tenant,

• then enter the date charged back to your account

• Enter "Returned Check Chargeback" & dollar amount

• Select proper Account "Rent Income", memo = description

• Select proper class, and finally select RECORD Button

If from Tenant, immediately go to TENANT TRACKING and enter NSF Check, NSF Fee, Late Charges, and Late Notice

Security Deposits

Many investors get totally bamboozled, confused and frustrated in dealing with a Tenant's Security Deposit because we are told this is not our money. This is your Tenant's money we are holding just in case they damage any of part of property above normal wear and tear....

THIS Language is probably from your LANDLORD/TENANT LAW and NOT the IRS!

The IRS does NOT give a flying rat's kahoona about your local landlord tenant law!

Now, knowing this right now.... When you get this money from your tenant, you will first enter it into your Tenant Tracking file and prepare a bank deposit summary and print it out.

Now, you go to your bank and physically make the bank deposit.

After returning to your office or home, you've got this Verified, and stamped deposit slip from your bank, and now it is time to enter this into your Investor Books. Here's what you do:

1) Open your Investor Books file

2) Click on the "DEPOSIT" Speed Button

3) Select the proper BANK ACCOUNT (Keep in mind, many landlord tenant laws do require the investor to have a separate bank account used exclusively for your tenants security deposits... if this is true, you will use this bank account)

4) Next enter the real date of the actual deposit... (you could have received their security deposit on Saturday, but didn't make it to the bank until Monday.)

5) In the Memo field, enter the address of the unit they rented.

6) TAB to the Account field and enter "RENTAL INCOME" account. Do NOT set this up into some kind of Liability account... this just makes things more cumbersome on your part...Siimply put, Report ALL of their security deposit as Rental Income.... When it gets refunded when they move out.... You will create a check and pull the same money from the RENTAL INCOME account. This works so much better than setting up a liability account. FYI, years ago, I did have it set up as a liability account and it was just so cumbersome and it actually costs more in tax preparation, especially if you are using any kiind of entities for tax benefits or asset protection...JUST USE THE KISS METHOD and report it all as rental income when you receive it.

OPTION MONEY

- **Many Investors pull their hair out on this one too.**
- **Let's keep it simple.**
- **USE YOUR IRA HAT HERE...**
- **Ask Yourself:**
  - **Did You Sell This Property?**
- **ANSWER IS NO!!! (not yet)**

Therefore, if you have not sold it yet... this means it probably is some kind of "investment" property you own or control. Either way, you probably are using IRS Schedule E to document INCOME and EXPENSES.

Hmm, look at the INCOME choices on Schedule E.... You've got RENTAL INCOME and ROYALTIES....

-Keep It Simple... REPORT ALL INCOME as You Get It.

-When You make a bank deposit into Investor Books from option money received from someone on one of your properties, simply deposit it into the proper bank account, and use the RENTAL INCOME Account for the option money deposit..

-On the class, use the property involved.

-HERE's SIMPLE PART... more times than not, the person who "purchased" the option to buy will not perform. At least this is my experience. Obviously, the larger the option fee, the better the odds of them actually following through and purchasing the property.

-So here's your real world results:

-If they fail to perform and do not exercise their option to buy, you have to do absolutely nothing because you've already entered it as Rental Income for the property involved. (fyi, just think how cumbersome and complicated it might be if you set up a liability account for their option money... these things just pile up because when they expire.... Yuk, it's just more work for YOU and this is not what we want... You want the KISS method.... I know because I've done it the wrong way and learned.)

- IF and when they exercise their option to buy and actually purchase the property... go back to your post office... simply "pull" their "option money" (if it is applied to purchase price) from the RENTAL INCOME account for the property involved. Of course, this might cause you to have a negative number for the tax year invvolved, but it is absolutely fine.

Creating CHECK to Tenant

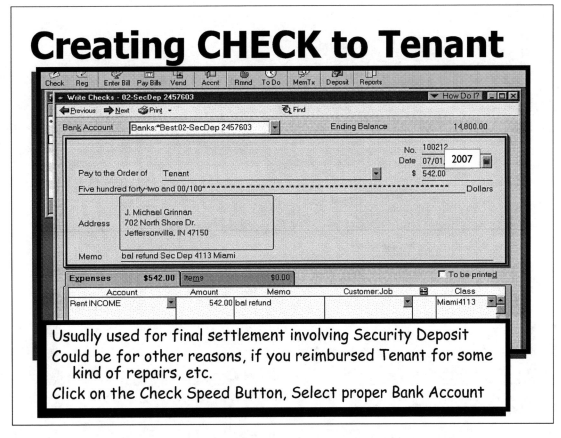

Usually used for final settlement involving Security Deposit
Could be for other reasons, if you reimbursed Tenant for some
kind of repairs, etc.
Click on the Check Speed Button, Select proper Bank Account

All of the Tenant detail is kept in TENANT TRACKING. No need to duplicate it.

"TENANT" is a vendor already set up for you in Investor Books.

Click on CREATE CHECK Speed Button

TAB thru fields entering proper data.

In the payee field enter TENANT

Change the address field to the Tenant name and address for mailing.

Remember the MEMO line and describe what this check involves.

TAB to each field and enter proper data, including CLASS

Creating CHECK to Tenant

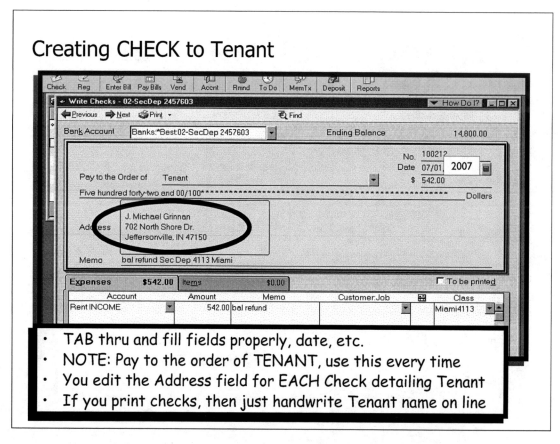

- TAB thru and fill fields properly, date, etc.
- NOTE: Pay to the order of TENANT, use this every time
- You edit the Address field for EACH Check detailing Tenant
- If you print checks, then just handwrite Tenant name on line

ALWAYS KEEP THE PAYEE FIELD **"TENANT"**

Simply change the name and address field as you TAB thru the fields while creating the check.

You can now use a window envelope and still have the data as to which Tenant received money.

MEMO lines, use them properly.

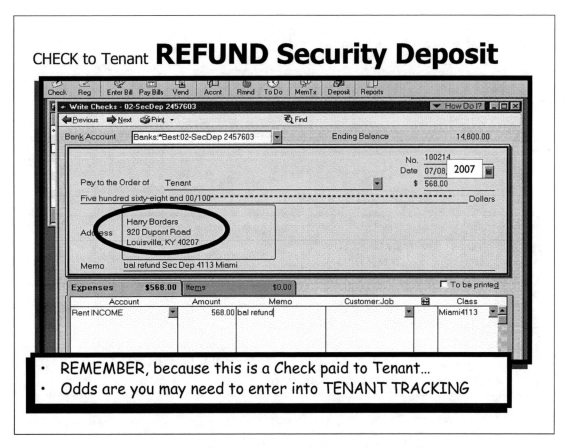

CHECK to Tenant **REFUND Security Deposit**

- REMEMBER, because this is a Check paid to Tenant...
- Odds are you may need to enter into TENANT TRACKING

Checks made payable to **TENANT** usually involve your tenant.

GO TO TENANT TRACKING and follow the proper steps to create a phantom check to be entered in the Tenant Register.

Yes, this is double work, but how often do you actually create a check to a tenant? .. Very seldom...don't complain, this system works.

REFUND SECURITY DEPOSIT: You will

determine the dollar amount to refund your tenant from your MOVE OUT REPORT prepared in your Tenant Tracking file. Once the dollar amount is known, simply create a check, just like above, made payable to "TENANT" and then enter their name, address, etc, in the address field.

Do NOT confuse this with your local landlord tenant law... Right now, you are wearing your Investor Hat and you are dealing with the IRS... Since you reported ALL of their Security Deposit as Rental Income when they moved in your rental unit..... Now, when you refund the balance due them, *(if any), you will pull it from your RENTAL INCOME account.

BUYING NOTES & Mortgages

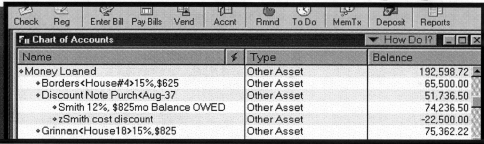

Name	⚡	Type	Balance
◆ Money Loaned		Other Asset	192,598.72
◆ Borders<House#4>15%,$625		Other Asset	65,500.00
◆ Discount Note Purch<Aug-37		Other Asset	51,736.50
◆ Smith 12%, $825mo Balance OWED		Other Asset	74,236.50
◆ zSmith cost discount		Other Asset	-22,500.00
◆ Grinnan<House18>15%,$825		Other Asset	75,362.22

- **Buying Discounted notes and mortgages**
- **Borrower still owes $74,236.50**
- **Noteholder agrees to sell note discounted $22,500.00**
- **Note is purchased for $51,736.50, but Borrower owes $74,236.50**

- **Structure your Money Loaned accounts as listed above.**
- **On Discounted Notes, create 2 subaccounts**
  - **1 subaccount shows the REAL BALANCE owed by Borrower**
  - **1 subaccount shows negative number reflecting discount.**
  - **Now, for Tax Purposes, your real cost basis is shown as balance.**

Sharp investors really do this stuff. The challenge is entering this new asset properly.

I am going to ignore the yields or rate or return, but just for example, let's use balance today on a note is $74,236.50 the BORROWER OWES. The loan victim is paying $625 per month on this loan. After I complete my "ciphering" on my HP12C (Hewlett Packard 12 C financial calculator, every investor should carry it) I determine I can pay $51,000 and some change and I will receive an annual interest acceptable to Mike.

Keep in mind here, if the borrower refinances or sells the property, even the day after I buy the mortgage, I will receive a check for $ 74,000 +.

The problem or challenge is how in the world do we enter this properly where it makes sense to me, my staff, my CPA. I learned the hard way one time when my office staff responded to a payoff requested and quoted $54,236.

Follow the name format and sub-account structured in the screen above to properly enter your discounted note and mortgage.

Your loan payments received will be recorded as INCOME INTEREST

One time annually, you will reduce the BORROWER's Balance by the amount of principal paid (if any) using the sub account of INCOME INTEREST.

1031 Tax Deferred Exchange

Regardless of the activity…

If You BRING Money
Start with a Check

If You Get Money
Start with a DEPOSIT

Since you are selling and you will be RECEIVING MONEY, (held by someone else), You will be making a Deposit into the

e1031 funds held Escrow Account.

Used by Investors to avoid paying Capital Gains Tax Now, you can defer it.
There are many variations involving 1031s including partials.
For KISS method purposes, example used will be simple and traditional.
• Investor has a house used for a rental for 10 years
• Investor purchased house 10 years ago for 50k
• Ballpark depreciation is $1,500 per year, reducing cost to 35k
• Investor can sell rental house for 140k resulting in 105k capital gain
• At 30% tax rate, could mean over 33k in Tax owed.
• Using the 1031 procedure PROPERLY, you could keep the 33k and roll it over into another like kind investment (1 or more rental houses)

We're NOT 1031 Experts,
but my attorney Harry Border is an Expert!
Call his office at 502-894-9200
Borders and Borders Attorneys
920 Dupont Road
Louisville, KY 40207
Objective: enter detail of the transaction(s) properly

200

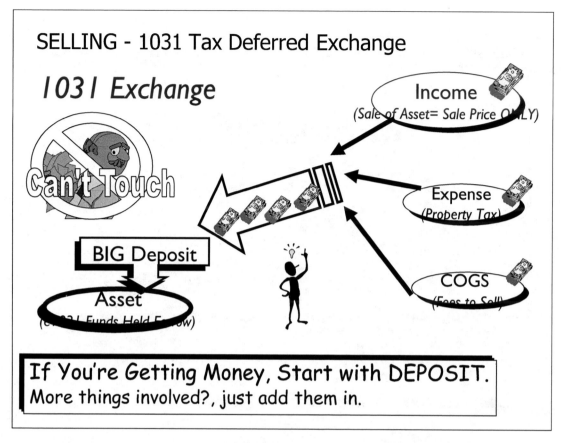

Here again, use a cartoon if it helps you.

You can NOT touch your money

Simply treat your e1031 Funds Held Escrow as a Bank Account.

It is your money held for a future purchase allowing you to roll over of DEFER your profit into your next bigger like kind investment.

1031 Tax Deferred Exchange

Name	⚡	Type	Balance
⬦Escrows		Other Current Asset	402.14 ▲
⬦e1031 funds held		Other Current Asset	0.00
⬦eBestBank		Other Current Asset	347.33
⬦e10023587<02nd745>Tax,Ins		Other Current Asset	49.69
⬦e10035687<Preston9620>Tax		Other Current Asset	297.64
⬦eWorstBank		Other Current Asset	54.81
⬦e802565<Burnett2217>Tax		Other Current Asset	630.42
⬦e803757<Miami4113>Ins		Other Current Asset	-575.61

Chart of Accounts ▼ How Do I?

A critical part of the 1031 process is the Seller can NOT touch any money from selling the investment.

Usually, the Seller will RECEIVE MONEY at closing = Start w/ Deposit

- **Click on Account Speed Button**
- **From Chart of Accounts Window**
- **Enter "e1031" and the e1031 funds held Account becomes highlighted**
- **double click it and open register.**

Since you will be receiving money at closing, go to your

e1031 funds held escrow account

and use it like a bank account.

Open it and start with a deposit.

ASK ABOUT REVERSE 1031 EXCHANGES where you can park a property on the shelf when you purchase it. If you happen to sell another property within 45 days your exchange is already set up. POWERFUL STRATEGY!

1031 Tax Deferred Exchange

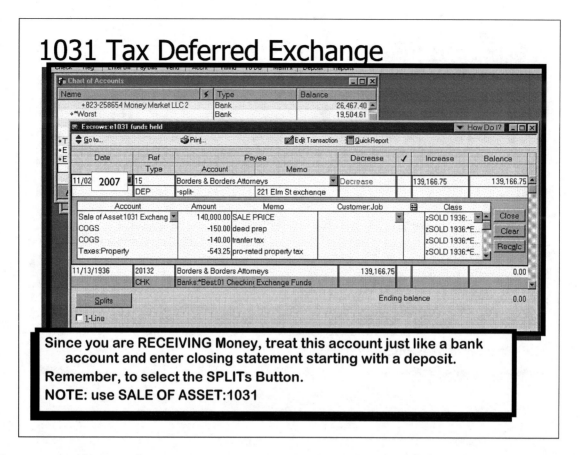

Since you are RECEIVING Money, treat this account just like a bank
account and enter closing statement starting with a deposit.

Remember, to select the SPLITs Button.

NOTE: use SALE OF ASSET:1031

Treat the closing statement just like any other sale except you will use

SALE OF ASSET:1031 EXCHANGE

In the first line for the Sale Price.

Everything with the closing statement is the same.

Such things as pro-ration of property taxes, Use COGS for expenses involved with selling the property including the intermediary fee.

1031 Tax Deferred Exchange

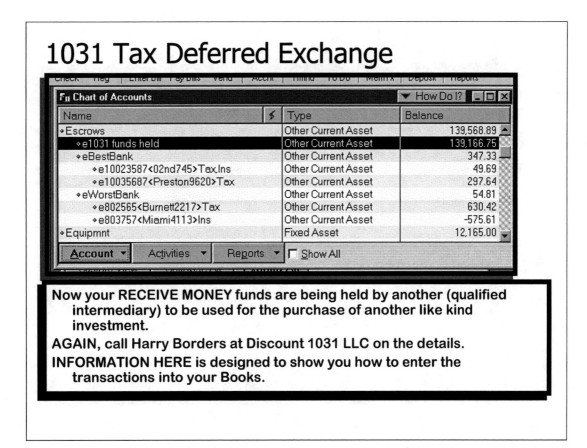

Name	⚡	Type	Balance
◆Escrows		Other Current Asset	139,568.89
◆e1031 funds held		Other Current Asset	139,166.75
◆eBestBank		Other Current Asset	347.33
◆e10023587<02nd745>Tax.Ins		Other Current Asset	49.69
◆e10035687<Preston9620>Tax		Other Current Asset	297.64
◆eWorstBank		Other Current Asset	54.81
◆e802565<Burnett2217>Tax		Other Current Asset	630.42
◆e803757<Miami4113>Ins		Other Current Asset	-575.61
◆Equipmnt		Fixed Asset	12,165.00

Now your RECEIVE MONEY funds are being held by another (qualified intermediary) to be used for the purchase of another like kind investment.

AGAIN, call Harry Borders at Discount 1031 LLC on the details.

INFORMATION HERE is designed to show you how to enter the transactions into your Books.

After completing the closing statement, you will see YOUR MONEY being held by the intermediary in your escrow account.

It is your money and will be reflected in your balance sheet as an asset.

In the future, if you successfully pull off the 1031, you make your purchase from the e1031 funds held escrow and treat it just like a bank again.

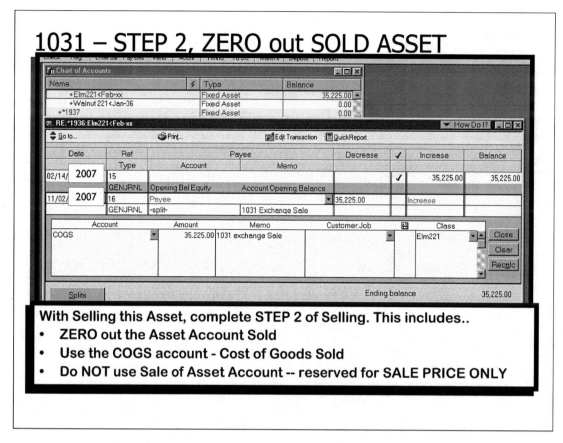

1031 – STEP 2, ZERO out SOLD ASSET

With Selling this Asset, complete STEP 2 of Selling. This includes..
- **ZERO out the Asset Account Sold**
- **Use the COGS account - Cost of Goods Sold**
- **Do NOT use Sale of Asset Account -- reserved for SALE PRICE ONLY**

You can not sell it and still own it.

ZERO out your asset account of the asset sold.

Use the COGS expense account.

Do NOT use SALE OF ASSET.

Always remember the class field.

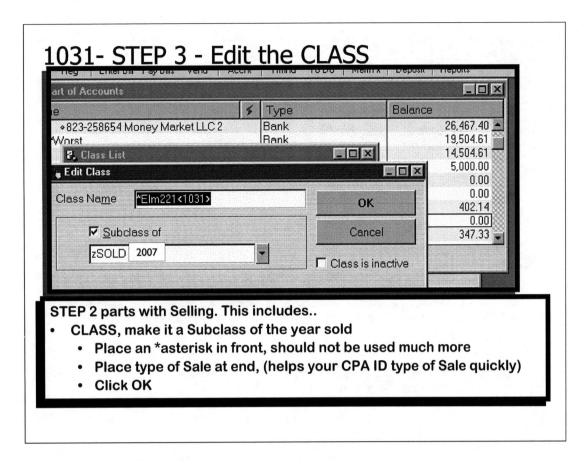

1031- STEP 3 - Edit the CLASS

STEP 2 parts with Selling. This includes..
- **CLASS, make it a Subclass of the year sold**
  - **Place an *asterisk in front, should not be used much more**
  - **Place type of Sale at end, (helps your CPA ID type of Sale quickly)**
  - **Click OK**

Edit the CLASS

Please an

> *Asterisk in front of the name

> **"1031"** at the end of name

And make the CLASS a subclass of the year sold.

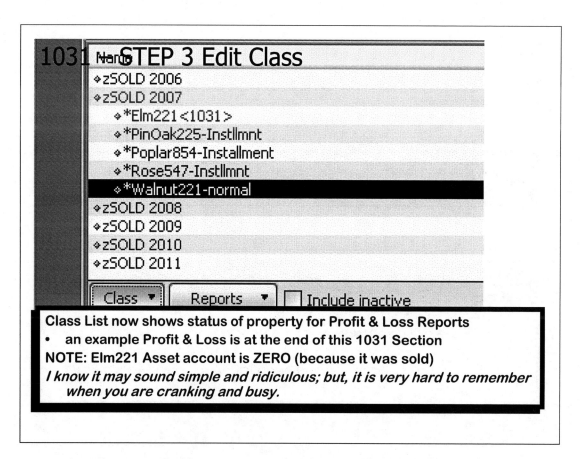

1031 **STEP 3 Edit Class**

- zSOLD 2006
- zSOLD 2007
  - *Elm221<1031>
  - *PinOak225-Instllmnt
  - *Poplar854-Installment
  - *Rose547-Instllmnt
  - *Walnut221-normal
- zSOLD 2008
- zSOLD 2009
- zSOLD 2010
- zSOLD 2011

Class ▼ | Reports ▼ | ☐ Include inactive

Class List now shows status of property for Profit & Loss Reports
- **an example Profit & Loss is at the end of this 1031 Section**

NOTE: Elm221 Asset account is ZERO (because it was sold)

I know it may sound simple and ridiculous; but, it is very hard to remember when you are cranking and busy.

Now the CLASS will appear in the year sold along with the type of sale involved.

207

1031 Tax Deferred Exchange – BUYING new Property

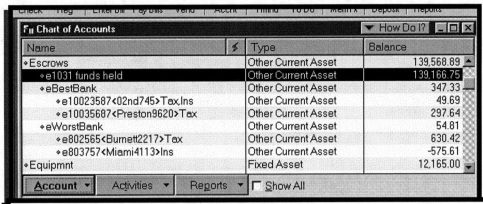

The clock is ticking… You have 45 days to Identify another property
Try to complete the purchase within 45 days makes it easier.
FINALLY, you have found a property to purchase -- SALE PRICE $165,000
You have $139,166.75 sitting in your 1031 account to use on this Exchange
Looks like you will be short some cash and need to bring money to closing

Use the e1031 funds escrow account just like the earnest money account.

The money sitting in this account will be used as part of the purchase money for buying a new asset.

208

1031 Tax Deferred Exchange – BUYING new Property

Regardless of the activity…

If You BRING Money
Start with a Check

If You Get Money
Start with a DEPOSIT

You find a property to purchase -- SALE PRICE $165,000
You have $139,166.75 sitting in your 1031 account to use on this Exchange
Looks like you will be short some cash and need to bring money to closing

Again, remember this phrase.

It works here too.

It is the universal rule.

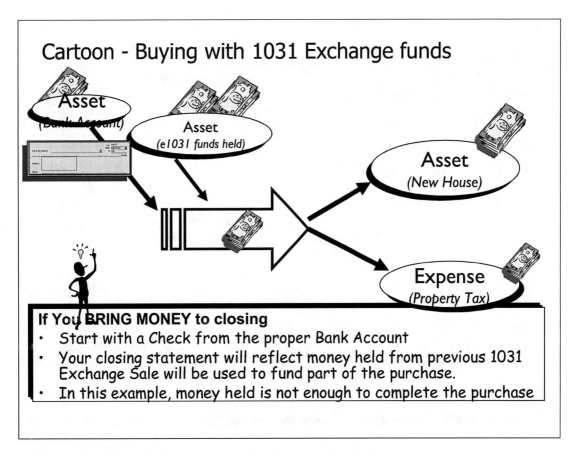

Cartoon - Buying with 1031 Exchange funds

Asset
(Bank Account)

Asset
(e1031 funds held)

Asset
(New House)

Expense
(Property Tax)

If You BRING MONEY to closing
- Start with a Check from the proper Bank Account
- Your closing statement will reflect money held from previous 1031 Exchange Sale will be used to fund part of the purchase.
- In this example, money held is not enough to complete the purchase

CARTOONS – use them if if helps you to understand and map out what is going on.

Add more variables if they are involved.

The example used involves bringing money to closing, so you will start with a check.

1031 Tax Deferred Exchange - Buying

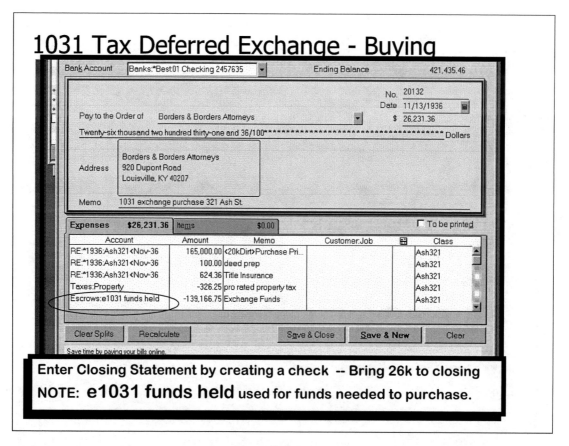

Click on CREATE CHECK speed button, select the proper bank account, and begin entering your closing statement.

You will pull funds from the e1031 funds held account to use as part of this purchase.

1031 Tax Deferred Exchange

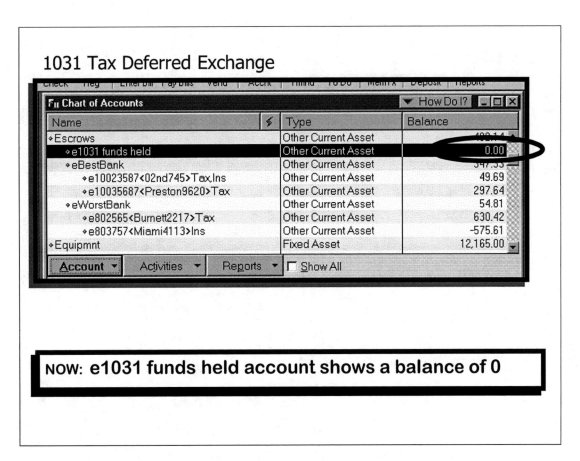

NOW: e1031 funds held account shows a balance of 0

After entering the closing statement properly, assuming you used all funds held, the balance in the e1031 funds held account will be zero.

1031 Tax Deferred Exchange

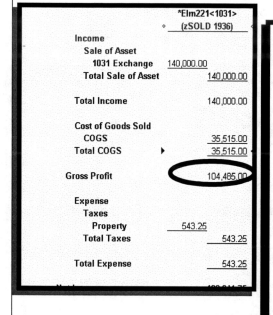

Profit & Loss Report

1031 objective is transferring the CAPITAL GAIN to the new property resulting in deferring the Tax until that property is sold.

1. Notice the CLASS Name at top
2. *Elm221<1031 Subclass of zSOLD 1936
3. Looks like CAPITAL GAIN of 104k - Equals Sale of Asset minus COGS
   - Do not include other income
   - if rent income is listed, deduct it from the gross profit number
1. This will reduce the COST BASIS in the new property by 104k
2. How to enter properly
   - Jot down number $104,485.00
   - Go to new property Asset Accnt

This is where some differences occur.

Remember, you are going to transfer the PROFIT of this property into the cost of the new property.

To help understand this process easy, let's review a Profit and Loss Report. After you sold the property to exchange, you edited the class name to appear as noted above.

Your Profit and Loss Report shows 104k as gross profit.

Take the gross profit amount MINUS Rent or other income, and jot it down somewhere – do it on this page if needed. You will use this number in a minute.

This number is the gross profit or CAPITAL GAIN subject to tax if not deferred properly in the 1031 process. The goal here is to move this gross profit from selling this investment into the new investment.

1031 Tax Deferred Exchange

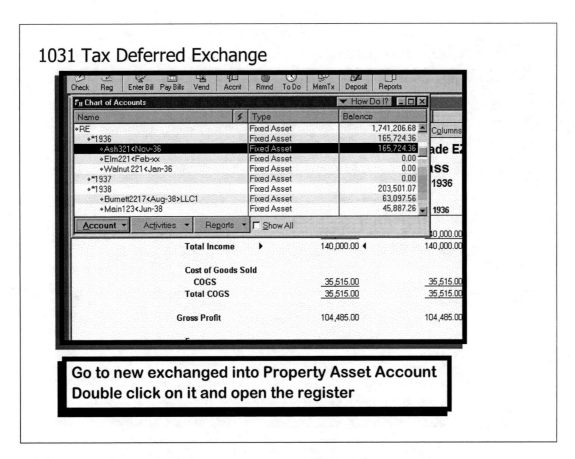

**Go to new exchanged into Property Asset Account
Double click on it and open the register**

Now go to the register of the just purchased new asset acquired.

1031 Tax Deferred Exchange

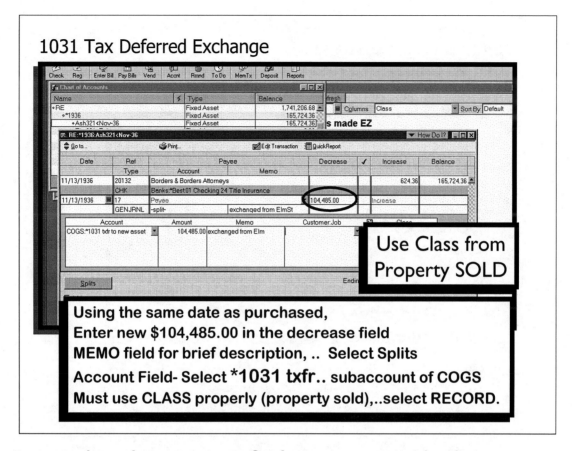

Remember the gross profit (minus rent and other income) number you just jotted down?

Use the same date as the purchase and DECREASE the balance in this asset account by the gross profit number.

Use the Sub Account of COGS called **"*1031 txfr"**

IMPORTANT:

You're using the Gross Profit Number from the SOLD PROPERTY; therefore you MUST use the class of the SOLD PROPERTY!

1031 Tax Deferred Exchange

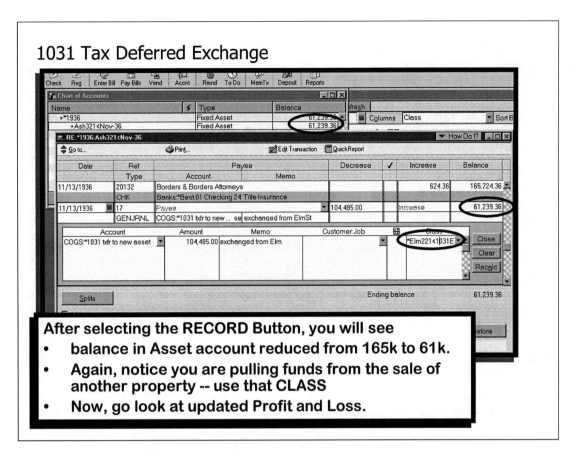

After selecting the RECORD Button, you will see
- balance in Asset account reduced from 165k to 61k.
- Again, notice you are pulling funds from the sale of another property -- use that CLASS
- Now, go look at updated Profit and Loss.

After selecting the RECORD Button, you will the balance (cost basis) in your new asset reduced by the amount of the gross profit of the sold property.

USE SOLD CLASS

Let's look at the Profit and Loss Report and how this procedure will effect your report for tax purposes.

This is probably the most important part of the 1031 procedure.

1031 Tax Deferred Exchange

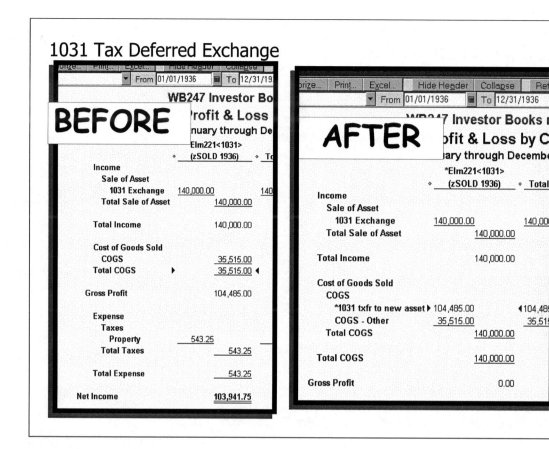

Study this for a moment.

BEFORE Report showed gross profit.

Because you reduced the balance in the new asset by pulling money from the sub account of COGS of the SOLD Property, you actually DEFERRED this gain to your new asset.

BINGO, you properly entered a 1031!

DEPRECIATION

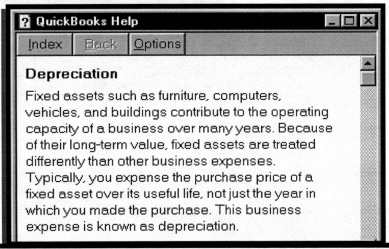

- I let my CPA handle this, but I determine value for DIRT
- MY CPA handles all Depreciation and keeps TAX Books for me
- Call your CPA to set up Depreciation in your QB
- I consider it very cumbersome, time consuming, and boring.

For real serious investors who insist on doing their own taxes and handling their own depreciation.

I recommend letting my real estate EXPERT CPA handle this for me.

If you insist, here is how to do it.

Above in the screen is QB Pro definition of Depreciation.

Involves Assets and Capital Improvements

It can be made into a very complicated and argumentative process when discussed or debated in a room full of EXPERTS.

For a Rule of Thumb,

• Residential property (houses) the improvement gets depreciated over 27.5 years.

• Commercial Property has another longer schedule.

• Capital Improvements to property have their own schedule that depends on the life of the improvement itself.

• I consider it a painful & time consuming process. I used to try to stay on top of it myself; however, I painfully discovered I was turning into a depreciation tracking expert instead of a successful real estate investor.

DEPRECIATION – Doing it Yourself

◈ HillcrestApts<Mar-39	Fixed Asset	877,811.00
◈ *1940	Fixed Asset	374,505.00
◈ 04th2628<Nov-40	Fixed Asset	125,837.00
◈ 24th525<Mar-40	Fixed Asset	65,287.00
◈ Miami4113<Apr-40	Fixed Asset	22,207.00
◈ Dirt<Miami	Fixed Asset	1,000.00
◈ Imprvmnt<Miami	Fixed Asset	21,207.00
◈ Fridge<Feb41>	Fixed Asset	0.00
◈ Furnace<Sept41>	Fixed Asset	0.00
◈ Roof<Mar41	Fixed Asset	0.00
◈ Oak509e<Aug-40	Fixed Asset	114,687.00
◈ Riv-Ridg-2354<Jan-40	Fixed Asset	46,207.00

- Fixed Asset Account Changes
- Each will have a Sub-Account for Dirt (Land Value) and for the Improvements. These are entered with the purchase closing statement. Land does NOT get depreciated, only the Improvements.

Some Investors insist on doing their own Taxes. Here are some helpful tips. This section is for advanced and/or experienced gurus.

Doing your own Depreciation will result in major changes to your Chart of Accounts involving your Fixed Assets.

BEFORE NOW, each property had it's own fixed asset account sorted by the year it was acquired.

Now, each Property (fixed asset) will have sub-accounts detailing the breakdown of each asset along with the improvements.

IMPORTANT – before jumping on the band wagon of doing this one your own, understand Depreciation is a Phantom Expense for Tax Purposes that actually **reduces** the COST BASIS of your investment.

•RULE of THUMB – PURPOSE – For example, if you purchase a refrigerator for $1,000 for an apartment, this would not be an EXPENSE for $1,000 for that property. Odds are, this would probably be a Capital Improvement to the Property. You would need to learn the "Life of the new Fridge." Suppose the life of the new Fridge is 10 years. This allows you to "depreciate" the cost of the $1,000 Fridge over 10 years and reducing the original Fridge asset by $100 each tax year. The fridge will be entered in your books as a $1,000 asset.. After the 1st year, the asset would be reduced to $900, etc.

Look at changes in Chart of Accounts as noted above in the screenshot.

DEPRECIATION – Doing it Yourself

◆ HillcrestApts<Mar-39	Fixed Asset	877,811.00
◆ *1940	Fixed Asset	374,505.00
◆ 04th2628<Nov-40	Fixed Asset	125,837.00
◆ 24th525<Mar-40	Fixed Asset	65,397.00
◆ Miami4113<Apr-40	Fixed Asset	22,207.00
◆ Dirt<Miami	Fixed Asset	1,000.00
◆ Imprvmnt<Miami	Fixed Asset	21,207.00
◆ Fridge<Feb41>	Fixed Asset	0.00
◆ Furnace<Sept41>	Fixed Asset	0.00
◆ Roof<Mar41	Fixed Asset	0.00
◆ Oak509e<Aug-40	Fixed Asset	114,687.00
◆ Bi...Rid...3254<...-40	Fixed Asset	46,397.00

Remember, Repairs made to the property BEFORE putting the property into service should be included as part of your acquisition cost...

Once the cost of the Depreciable Asset has been determined, you can set up the automatic depreciation of the Asset.

A major change involves setting your asset account when you purchase a property.

You will create:

new FIXED ASSET

     sub - DIRT

     sub - IMPRVMNTs (improvements)

       sub of each Capitalized Expense

(The big frustration to me is my cost basis of each fixed asset will be reduced monthly with automatic entry of depreciation)

DEPRECIATION – Doing it Yourself

◆ HillcrestApts<Mar-39	Fixed Asset	877,811.00
◆ *1940	Fixed Asset	374,505.00
◆ 04th2628<Nov-40	Fixed Asset	125,837.00
◆ 34th525s<Mar-40	Fixed Asset	65,387.00
◆ Miami4113<Apr-40	Fixed Asset	22,207.00
◆ Dirt<Miami	Fixed Asset	1,000.00
◆ Imprvmnt<Miami	Fixed Asset	21,207.00
◆ Fridge<Feb41>	Fixed Asset	0.00
◆ Furnace<Sept41>	Fixed Asset	0.00
◆ Roof<Mar41	Fixed Asset	0.00
◆ Oak509e<Aug-40	Fixed Asset	114,687.00
◆ Rizz Ridge 2254<Jan-40	Fixed Asset	46,207.00

Let's Do an Example of a New Roof installed the tax year after the property was purchased.
ROOF COST $4,500
- guesstimate of life of New Roof is 15 years
- $4,500 divided by 15 years = $300 annual
    - resulting in $25.00 monthly depreciation

Above list an example of capitalizing a roof expense.

Create Check for $4,500 using "Capitalized" for the proper class.

You MUST use the Capitalized Expense Account or your P&L or Cash Flow Report will be worthless.

DEPRECIATION – Doing it Yourself

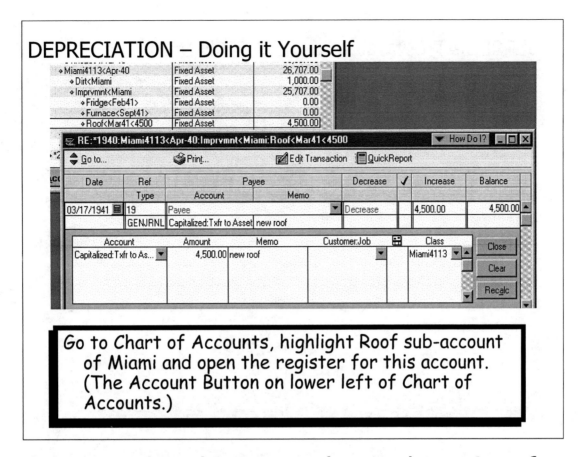

Go to Chart of Accounts, highlight Roof sub-account of Miami and open the register for this account. (The Account Button on lower left of Chart of Accounts.)

Click Accnt Speed Button and open the register for the new fixed asset sub account you just created for this new roof.

TAB thru and enter the proper data in each field and INCREASE the balance in this account by the amount of the roof cost.

must use the SPLITS button to enter the class.

In the Account Field, **use the sub account of CAPITALIZED Expense account Txfrd to Asset** and remember to enter the proper class.

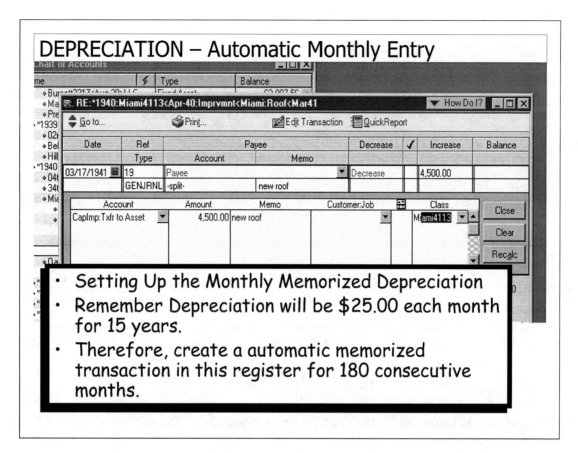

DEPRECIATION – Automatic Monthly Entry

- Setting Up the Monthly Memorized Depreciation
- Remember Depreciation will be $25.00 each month for 15 years.
- Therefore, create a automatic memorized transaction in this register for 180 consecutive months.

Setting up automatic monthly entries of all depreciation is easy.

GROUND RULE: pick and use the same date each month for all depreciation entries. This example uses the 17th of each month.

Remember, You must CREATE a transaction first BEFORE you can memorize it.

Using the example above, TAB thru and create a transaction DECREASING the balance by $25.00 using the DEPRECIATION Expense account and the proper class.

Do NOT select the Record Button, You must memorize it by Selecting EDIT on Tool Bar, and MEMORIZE entry.

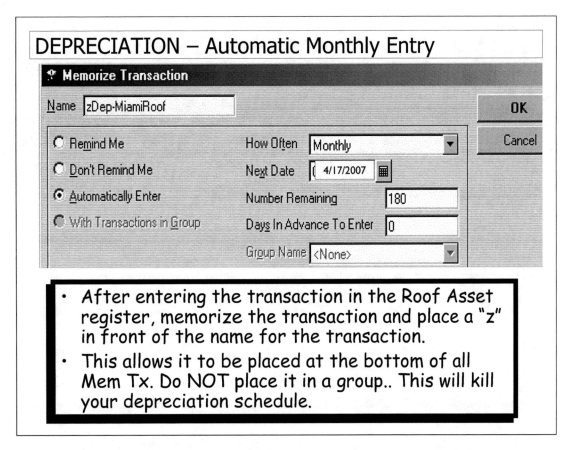

DEPRECIATION – Automatic Monthly Entry

Memorize Transaction

Name zDep-MiamiRoof

OK

Cancel

- Remind Me
- Don't Remind Me
- Automatically Enter
- With Transactions in Group

How Often: Monthly

Next Date: 4/17/2007

Number Remaining: 180

Days In Advance To Enter: 0

Group Name: <None>

- After entering the transaction in the Roof Asset register, memorize the transaction and place a "z" in front of the name for the transaction.
- This allows it to be placed at the bottom of all Mem Tx. Do NOT place it in a group.. This will kill your depreciation schedule.

MEMORIZE TRANSACTION window will appear.

Set this up for automatic entry each month.

Name the transaction with something to make sense to you and place a small Z in front of the name. This will keep all depreciation memorized transactions together.

TAB to and Select Automatically Enter.

TAB to and Select MONTHLY

TAB to and Select next date (17th)

TAB to and Select number of schedule monthly entries for the depreciating asset.

ALWAYS Select ZERO for days in advance to enter.

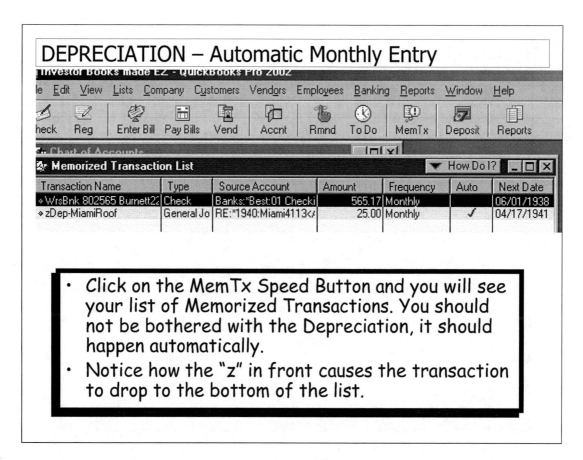

DEPRECIATION – Automatic Monthly Entry

> - Click on the MemTx Speed Button and you will see your list of Memorized Transactions. You should not be bothered with the Depreciation, it should happen automatically.
> - Notice how the "z" in front causes the transaction to drop to the bottom of the list.

Click on MemTx Speed Button to see your list of Memorized Transactions to insure your depreciation entry has been entered.

Place a small "**z**" in front of all of your depreciation memorized transactions in order to allow for proper sorting and list them all together at the END of your memorized transaction list.

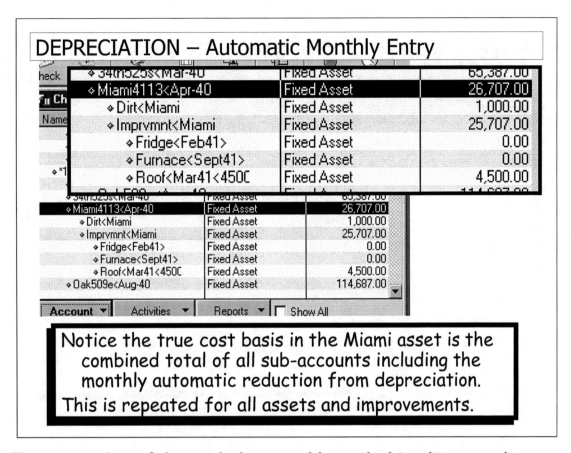

DEPRECIATION – Automatic Monthly Entry

◇ 34th525s<Mar-40	Fixed Asset	65,387.00
◇ Miami4113<Apr-40	Fixed Asset	26,707.00
◆ Dirt<Miami	Fixed Asset	1,000.00
◆ Imprvmnt<Miami	Fixed Asset	25,707.00
◆ Fridge<Feb41>	Fixed Asset	0.00
◆ Furnace<Sept41>	Fixed Asset	0.00
◆ Roof<Mar41<450C	Fixed Asset	4,500.00

◇ 34th525s<Mar-40	Fixed Asset	65,387.00
◇ Miami4113<Apr-40	Fixed Asset	26,707.00
◆ Dirt<Miami	Fixed Asset	1,000.00
◆ Imprvmnt<Miami	Fixed Asset	25,707.00
◆ Fridge<Feb41>	Fixed Asset	0.00
◆ Furnace<Sept41>	Fixed Asset	0.00
◆ Roof<Mar41<450C	Fixed Asset	4,500.00
◇ Oak509e<Aug-40	Fixed Asset	114,687.00

Account ▼ | Activities ▼ | Reports ▼ | ☐ Show All

> Notice the true cost basis in the Miami asset is the
> combined total of all sub-accounts including the
> monthly automatic reduction from depreciation.
> This is repeated for all assets and improvements.

The examples of depreciation used intended to show you how to use QB to handle your depreciation. You and your CPA must determine what the life of the improvement or schedule to use.

ADVANCED USERS may elect to do their own depreciation.

IMPORTANT – remember, Depreciation is an expense account and this will and can greatly effect your Profit and Loss Reports.

If you wish to make a true "Cash Flow Report", you must modify the the Cash Flow Report and remove the sub-account of Capitalized Expense and Depreciation Expense; otherwise it will be useless as a cash flow report because it will be a tax summary report instead.

Year End - THINGS TO DO

1. Enter Principal paid on all loans
   - Mortgages with 1098 info in Memo field
   - Installment Sales
2. Create Profit & Loss by Class Report
3. ZERO Out Capitalized Expenses - Txfr to Asset
4. Review Properties Sold
5. CLASSES - make sure properly labeled
6. Review Chart of Accounts - look for weird stuff.
7. Let QB create 1099's for Vendors
8. Create 1098's for mortgage loan customers
9. Create & Save 1096 (1098 & 1099 Summary Reports)

Assuming your tax year ends on Dec 31, you can do the above sometime in January at your leisure.

QB will create your 1099s.

Click on VENDOR Speed Button.

Click on Vendor Button and select Print 1099. Follow the steps and QB will do it for you. Remember, your vendor must be set up properly with address, tax id, and the 1099 box checked in order to get them on your list of 1099s.

Prepare a Profit and Loss Report for the Tax Year and MEMORIZE IT into the list of memorized transactions for the year involved.

STUDY it carefully. Look for weird stuff, look at the CLASS COLUMN of UNCLASSIFIED. It should be ZERO. If it has entries, simply double click on the dollar amount, go to it and correct it by entering the proper class.

Review your classes and make sure the sold properties and named correctly.

www.MikeButler.com

Year End - Principal Pay Downs

Use Quicken for actual Loan Tracking if you do not trust your Lender. I do not trust them and I use Quicken.

1. You will or should receive 1098 at the end of year from Lender.
2. Sometimes you will not receive 1098's from Lender.
3. First, compare 1098 and their balances to your balances.
4. Go to Liability Loan Account register one at a time.
   - Open the register and enter the last day of the year
   - Decrease your Mortgage Loan balance by the principal amount paid for the year.
   - Enter Mortgage Interest: Principal Paid as the Account
   - MEMO field "1098 = whatever they reported as mtg interest"
     1. Remember MEMO field explains to your CPA
     2. Used properly you can file all 1098s and not give them to your CPA for extra billing.
5. Repeat same process for your Loan Customers & refer to Installment Sales procedures for EZ year end steps.

Follow the steps above for principal paid on each of your mortgage loans.

Repeat this procedure for each of your loan customers (victims) using the principal paid sub account of INCOME INTEREST.

This also includes properties you sold using the INSTALLMENT SALES.

Year End - 1st Step with CPA

AFTER CAREFUL REVIEW

1. Schedule Appt with your CPA
2. Print 2 Profit & Loss by Property Reports
3. Print 2 Balance Sheet showing all balances.
4. Along with 1096's.
5. Take these 4 Reports with you for an review meeting before pulling the trigger.
6. Most of the time, minor changes are needed
7. You will find errors, (purpose of the review)
8. Go back home or to office and make the changes, and finally....

After careful review as noted on the previous pages, schedule an appointment with your tax preparer or CPA.

TAKE 2 REPORTS (2 copies) with You

1.) Profit & Loss by Class for tax year

2.) Balance Sheet as of the last day of the tax year showing previous year balance in a 2nd column.

Together, review your reports. Both of you will find additional errors. Note them directly on the reports and go back home or to your office and make the corrections.

NOW you can burn a CD or email to your CPA.

Year End - Last Step with CPA

1. Make a back-up Copy
2. E-mail to your CPA or back up to Disk and deliver or mail them to your CPA...

STOP hauling sacks, boxes, files, closing statements, checks, receipts, etc.

Get back to Business & Fun!

This is what it is all about, making this painful and boring subject an effective efficient REAL ESTATE INVESTMENT TOOL for YOU!!

It really works.

Each year will build on the next.

You can see your results of any date range with just a few clicks.

Make it do MORE – Things You should learn.

Learn to
- FILTER your Reports
- Memorize and SAVE your favorite Reports.
- Review this year compared to last year on both balance sheets and profit and loss

Filter Reports – with any report displayed, click on the "MODIFY" button in the upper left corner. This allows you to change the parameters of the report. Such things as dates, properties involved, accounts, etc. This is powerful.

MEMORIZE and save your favorite reports. If you discover you like a particular report, especially a report you have to modify and filter, memorize and save it for future use. It will be saved in the list of memorized reports for future use.

DEVELOP GOOD BUSINESS HABITS and review your balance sheets and profit and loss reports on a regular basis. Also include Year to Date compared to last year. Although it is difficult to do the first year, as your system grows it will become amazingly powerful. See your rents increase or decrease and see how much you are spending on advertising, telephones, insurance, property taxes, etc.

Make it do MORE – Things You should learn.

Learn to

- Develop good business habits.
- Set up your own in house escrows for taxes and insurance.
- Join Cranking It 24-7, become a member now.

POWERFUL TIP: I do not trust lenders with my money in escrow accounts for taxes and insurance. So many times, I hear investors say it is so much easier to let the lender handle it. THEY SCREW IT UP. If you took advantage of the easy 30 year money in recent years, the annual adjustment to your monthly payment due to the escrow adjustment just shoots down the benefit of having it automated.

SET UP YOUR OWN IN HOUSE ESCROW FOR TAXES AND INSURANCE. It's easy. Go to the bank and open a money market account. They will give you checks, you earn interest, and are allowed to make 3 withdrawals a month. Create this bank account as an "other asset" and make this bank account a sub-account of your escrow accounts and create an automatic monthly payment to this bank account for 1/12th of your annual property tax and insurance expense.

CRANKING IT 24-7 **memberships for real estate investors! Become a SILVER, GOLD, or PLATINUM Member Today at www.CrankingIt.com**

232

Common Questions & Answers

Q: I already have Quickbooks. Will it work on regular Quickbooks? You must have Quickbooks Pro 2002, Quickbooks Pro 2003, Quickbooks Pro 2004, or Quickbooks Pro 2005, Quickbooks Pro 2006 or newer to work properly. It will NOT work on Quickbooks basic. It works fine on Quickbooks PREMIER. Additionally, it doesn't work on the special flavors of Quickbooks such as "contractor version" or Legal version.

Q: But I already use Quickbooks. How do I get all of my stuff and data into this system Mike? Reality check. Unfortunately, I don't know any investor who has successfully imported or exported "data" into Quickbooks Pro. I know many experts say you can. I've tried, and I know many others who've tried with no luck. I have yet to find one person who has successfully pulled this off. The ANSWER: You have two choices:

      1.) The simplest answer is to pick a "STARTING DATE", preferably a tax year like Jan 1. Use your Fast Start Guide to get up and running right now fast. Using a start date allows you an easy mark to simply say "Everything before this date is in my old system, and everything from this date forward is in my new system." Hold on, don't freak out. Read on

Q: But I want ALL of my data in one set of books. Me too. This is what is beautiful about Quickbooks. You can enter data BACKWARDS in QB PRO. For example, let's say today is May 9 and you get your Investor Books up and running. You're paying bills and making deposits; however, you want all of your transactions back to January 1 of this year in your Investor Books. No problem. Take a rainy Saturday morning and enter a month at a time using the real dates of each transaction. Here's a sneaky short cut tip. Create a PHANTOM BANK ACCOUNT to use for all of those transactions you enter prior to the May 9 example. Let's say your actual up and running date is May 9. At your leisure, using the PHANTOM Bank account, simply go into the phantom bank account register and enter each transaction as they really occurred .. Real date, real check number, etc.

<u>Existing Quickbooks Users – The transition is your biggest challenge.</u> Driving it daily is Easy, Your transition is your challenge, but this happens only one time and you're done.

Q: Tenant's Security Deposits… Where do they go? Odds are, many states have a landlord/tenant law requiring landlords to deposit the tenant's security or damage deposit into a separate bank account used exclusively for this purpose. **NOTE: Your state's landlord/tenant law has nothing to do with the IRS.** Do you see "security deposit" on the IRS Form Schedule E? Absolutely not. Use the Kiss method. As you enter the bank deposit to the bank account involving the tenant's security deposit, report it as Rental Income for the property involved. Don't freak out, yes, it's the tenant's money you're holding. You are in compliance with your state's landlord tenant law. They don't tell you how to report it for TAX PURPOSES, they tell you to keep it separate. My CPA informed me to report it as Rental Income and if and when I create a check to tenant to refund all or part of their security deposit, I once again, pull it from the Rent Income account for the property involved. My CPA stated it's just more complicated and expensive to track their security deposit as a liability account.

233

Common Questions & Answers

Q: I do Lease/Options. Where do I put the Tenant's Option Money? Once again, don't beat yourself and make this complicated.

       - Do You See Option Income on the IRS Form Schedule E? NO

       - Have You SOLD the Property? NO

- Keep It Simple…. **Report your Option money as RENT INCOME for property involved.** Don't freak out again… If and when your tenant exercises their "Option To Buy" you'll simply pull the amount of "option money" from the Rent Income account for the property involved.

Q: My accountant or CPA wants me to give my "books" or file to them and wait till they get done "cleaning it up" or editing. How do I operate, pay bills and make deposits while they are doing this?

      -Rule #1 – They work for YOU.

      -Rule #2 – This is your tool to drive your business. An Added Benefit for you is how this program gathers all of your data and produces clean, nice Tax Summary Reports your tax preparer can understand.

      - You Operate this system day and day out in your investing business.

      - You make a copy of your file and give it to your tax preparer, accountant or CPA. They take your file and tweak it till their heart is content, **BUT LET THEM KEEP IT**. If they try to give you an "updated file" to use, just tell them "that's OK, you keep it."

      - Repeat this same process next year, and the next year and so on.

      - You do not need to understand all of the stuff they want to enter. You're simply giving them good solid data to prepare your taxes in an efficient and inexpensive manner.

      -Rule #3 – Ask your Tax Preparer to give you your tax return in PDF format and you can create a folder for each year Tax Returns on your computer in "My Documents" to begin a collection of your tax returns. I've discovered this is a very good practice as my CPA amends returns forward and backwards and it's just simply hard to keep all of the "paper" together.

Good Luck and Happy Investing!

Mike Butler

Resources

www.LandlordingOnAutoPilot.com is an absolute must for real estate investors today. Written by Mike Butler, this 256 page book published by John Wiley and Sons shows you exactly how Mike managed 75 rental properties while working his full time job as an undercover cop. PLUS you dozens of FREE Forms you can customize in Microsoft Word.

www.CrankingIt247.com is the monthly publication for investors. Get a 30 Day FREE Silver Membership!

CYA – Protecting Your ASSets is a 3 hour Seminar showing investors the simple, not complicated and cost effective asset protection program. No need for out of state entities or off-shore bank accounts. Mike Butler and attorney Harry Borders will show you this simple program for investors. It includes a manual, forms, over 3 hours of audio cds, and a forms CD. Call 800-895-4373 or online at www.MikeButler.com

TAX Concerns and Strategies for Today's Real Estate Investor: a live seminar workshop, over 3 hours professionally recorded, presented by Mike Butler and his personal CPA, Mike Grinnan of McCauley Nicolas and Co LLC accounting firm. Forced to speak in investor friendly language Mike and Mike explain in our language, good, solid, tax saving strategies for the beginner, intermediate, and advanced investor. This course includes a manual, 3 audio cds and a forms cd PLUS a 1on1 private tax consultation. Call 800-895-4373.

Home Study Courses for Investors Your "University on Wheels" allows you to learn while you roll in your travels. Visit **www.MikeButler.com**

www.Landlordlocks.com will save and make you money! Call Ernie Riddle at 800-847-8729

1031 Tax Deferred Exchange, do your next one with attorney **Harry Borders** of Borders and Borders Attorneys. Phone: 502-894-9200 and Harry's email is Hborders@aol.com. Be sure to ask about **REVERSE Exchanges.**

Yard Signs, Banners – www.BanditSigns.com Call 877-877-8664 and tell David Alexander Mike Butler sent ya'

FREE Business Cards – www.VistaPrint.com (No relationship to Vista Properties, Inc)

~~www.MikeButlerLoans.com~~